TENNIS:
Beyond the Inner Game

Craig R. Wilson

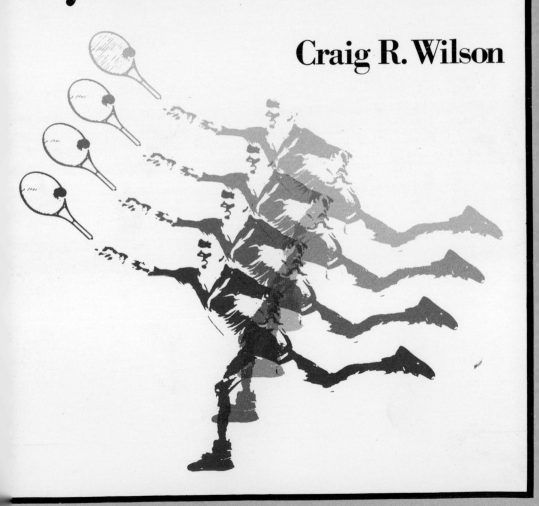

TENNIS:

Beyond the Inner Game

Also by Craig R. Wilson

HOW TO IMPROVE YOUR TENNIS:
Style, Strategy, Analysis

THE TENNIS PLAYER'S PROFILE

THE PLAYER INTERACTION ANALYSIS

TENNIS:
Beyond the Inner Game

Craig R. Wilson

Drake Publishers Inc
New York • London

ACKNOWLEDGEMENTS

Susan Soper . . . for her friendship and editorial advice.

Dr. L. Craig Wilson, my father, for his encouragement through the years, his invaluable editorial advice, and his constant inspiration.

Rick Devereux Jr., my closest friend, who shared the ideas, and who was an instrumental force in the development of this project from the beginning. We played and taught the mental game together.

My children, since it was from them that I learned about the concept of "childlikeness," its simplicity and its beauty . . . Tonya, Craig, and Mark.

Z. Mincek, friend and co-worker during the writing of the original manuscript . . . a straight shooter.

All of the Ponte Vedra "tennis ladies", Ponte Vedra Beach, Fla.

Helen Ely, for her typing of the final manuscript.

Published in 1977 by
Drake Publishers Inc.
801 Second Avenue
New York, N.Y. 10017

TENNIS: Beyond the Inner Game
LC: 76-27798

ISBN: 0-8473-1361-1

Printed in the United States of America

Contents

DEDICATION

To my mother, Helen Nunez Wilson
. . . with love.

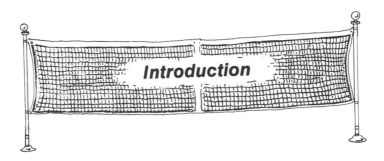

Introduction

This book is about the people who play tennis—those who do it well, and also those who settle for less but still feel they got their money's worth.

There is some satire, maybe even a little sarcasm, reflecting the kind of people who are attracted to the game. But also there is an underlying seriousness derived from the notion that self-mastery is a lifelong pursuit which can take place in any medium which taxes the human spirit. One such challenge is tennis.

Thus, we are primarily concerned with people and secondarily with the game. The book's title, *Tennis: Beyond the Inner Game*, takes certain liberties with the meditative approach to life which popular belief calls to mind. Yet, it is not a total travesty since the greatest margin for improvement in almost anybody's game is, in fact, his "inner game"— the structure of motivation, value, and social interaction which provides the foundation for physical skill.

There is something unique about the non-contact personal sport which pits one player against another on an assumed parity but from the very first service attempts to make a myth of the idea of equality. No matter how good a player gets—even world class—there is always someone else just a bit better. Also, there is the ever-present threat that a player's peak performance has slipped into the past, never again to be recaptured.

Even so, a tennis player does not have to stop playing when age, distraction, or a shortage of suitable partners makes unrealistic his earlier olympic ambitions. Indeed, the polite social setting of tennis causes many people to begin and end with a fascination with the "tennis life-style," victories or defeats being only incidental happenings of no more—or no less—importance than who said what to whom at the last cocktail party. People of all ages play the game and their motives vary as much as their skill; however, they all want to do their best and that elusive "best" is hidden within, always resisting full release. Even a casual visit to a tennis club (especially the pro-shop) reveals the propor-tion of the clientele which represents the enthusiastic beginner (clinics are big business), and the assertive modern woman (who takes most of the private lessons). Mixed doubles at various points, becomes both a dating game and a family diversion. Weaving his or her way through this intricate leisure life-style is the serious competitor with a possible career commitment to the game. It all adds up to a complex social system, unlike, say, basketball, requiring more than a pair of sneakers to crash the gate.

Tennis: Beyond the Inner Game thus begins with a hypothetical mixed doubles match in which the private thoughts of the participants, some quite unrelated to the immediate game, become the controlling factors in success, or the lack of it. Appropriate life-style generalizations are drawn from the example and attention then shifts to the "psychology of self-transcendancy." Finally, well-known world class players—both past and present—are characterized in light of the criterion of the inner game. The portraits are not free of gossip, but stop short of libel as the complicated motivations of the very best players are deduced from the factual records of their brilliant achievements. After the fashion of the TV broadcasters, both the "ecstacy" and the "agony" of obsessive suc-cess are permitted to become part of the story. Illustrations, both nar-rative and photographic, try to capture the champion in his natural habitat. All that remains is for the reader to put himself into the picture.

Craig R. Wilson

Part I

THE SOCIAL SMOKESCREEN

CHAPTER 1

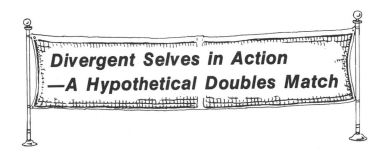

Divergent Selves in Action
—A Hypothetical Doubles Match

The following discussion and dialogue is meant to take the form of a typical club level mixed doubles match. Each of the participants has been deliberately chosen to typify four of the most common selves that characterize the game, any club, Anywhere U.S.A. Our participants include the following cast:

1. Exaggerate—the exaggerated self, male, married to his partner, Sylvia Self Limit. He will try and carry her in the game of tennis in the same way he sees himself compensating for her in the game of life.

2. Sylvia Self Limit—the self-limiting self, she seeks compensation from Exaggerate. She identifies with a strength she feels she lacks.

3. Patricia Prettiness—not married to her partner, Tommy Transcendental. She hand-picked him, however, because he looks good, he has his head together, as they say, and she likes being a part of that image.

4. Tommy Transcendental—the transcendental ideal self, believes in himself, confident, playing this particular match primarily to amuse himself. He will not worry about the outcome, his self image is not threatened here, he doesn't concern himself

with the social gossip of the club. This match does not hold the same social import for him that it does for the others.

The Night Before

The mixed doubles championship of Anyclub was a weekend affair that stretched over two weekends. Friday was a rather undistinguished day at the office for Exaggerate. He could have gotten more done, but he was looking forward to his regular poker game that night where he could discuss his upcoming match with his non-tennis playing friends. "Discuss" is probably an inadequate description; predict, vicariously analyze the weaknesses of the opposition (and his strengths) would probably be more accurate. Sylvia Self Limit was also preoccupied that day. She found it hard to concentrate on her soap operas, she took an emergency lesson from the local pro, a Valium with her dinner and two Excedrin P.M.'s at bedtime. Exaggerate came tiptoeing in at 2 a.m. He knew he drank more than the ordinary man could handle and still play well, but he was the class of the field and nothing could or would alter that. Self Limit sleeps on.

Patricia Prettiness prepared for her match by getting her hair fixed and buying a new tennis dress. She was going to look right out there. Tommy Transcendental spent Friday night alone, listening to his stereo and reading *Atlas Shrugged* by Ayn Rand. He only thought of the match once and when he did he merely smiled to himself and turned to the next page.

That Morning

Exaggerate woke up with a headache, a hangover to be more precise. He fixed himself a Bloody Mary to neutralize the beer of the night before and bumped into Sylvia Self Limit as he entered the bathroom to brush his teeth. Self Limit was there to get another tranquilizer but said "good morning" in the steadiest voice she could muster. She tells Exaggerate how good he looks since, after all, he was her only hope. He knows he feels bad but decides maybe she was right after all, that his innate greatness was again showing itself, that even at his worst he was still superior. Patrician Prettiness woke up early, took a hot bath in oil and bubbles and spent considerable time assembling her tennis bag with towels, wristbands and a Gatorade. Transcendental woke up as he always did, poured himself a glass of orange juice and read the paper according to his customary morning ritual.

Prior to the Match

The match was scheduled for 9:30 a.m. Exaggerate was ready to play at 8:30, however, dragging Self Limit away from her bible of life, MIRACLES ARE REAL, insisting that she cram for the match on the way to the courts. They arrived on the scene at 8:45, only forty-five minutes until showtime. Exaggerate paced the floor, repeatedly looking to the door of the clubhouse for the opposition. When his opposition failed to fill his vision, he looked for his poker buddies, for his friends and fans. He couldn't believe that Transcendental and Patricia weren't as anxious to hit the courts as he was, but then the longer they delayed, the longer they could vicariously indulge themselves in the possibility, but surely not the probability, of victory. Sylvia disappeared for awhile, going to the ladies' room to towel off from her typical cold sweat of anticipation. When she returned to the lobby, she receded into a corner of the pro shop hidden by racks of dresses, meditating, imagining the headlines that would surely appear in the morning paper, *"Self Limit a Load Too Heavy Even For Exaggerate—They lose 6−0, 6−0."* Prettiness was the next to arrive. She calculated her appearance for exactly 9:15 so that her new tennis finery, not to mention her innate beauty, could be on display for exactly fifteen minutes—just enough to whet the appetites of the envious. Transcendental strolled in at 9:25 wearing the same warm-up he always did, his hair uncombed and without dry look spray, carrying his shoes in hand, walking softly, stocking feet and all.

The Procession to the Court

The players received the new can of balls from their pro and proceeded through the crowd to court number one. Exaggerate led the way of course, back arched, head high. Greatness was about to enter its element. He quickly hid his left hand from view, however, when he realized belatedly that he had cut his finger on the top of the can after opening it with more than a little enthusiasm. Self Limit noticed, shuddered to herself, and wondered how their luck could be so bad as to injure his tossing hand today. Patricia Prettiness didn't notice since, at the time, she was busy admiring her reflection in the plate glass window of the clubhouse. Transcendental followed the pack still tying his shoelaces and carrying his single racket, no cover, under his arm. Exaggerate had three rackets, new gut the day before. He never did understand how that clod Transcendental could possibly think he could compete on this level with that war club. One racket was bad enough, but one as worn and used as that one was just too much.

The Warm-Up

The teams assumed the traditional line-up, men on the backhand side, women on the forehand. Exaggerate warmed-up with Prettiness, Self Limit with Transcendental. Exaggerate bounced the balls at a rapid pace as he trotted to the baseline. Once there, he dropped the ball and hit a beautiful topspin drive right past Patricia. Yes, this was going to be a good day. Exaggerate's self-indulgence was fine with Patricia, however, since the ball did land near the fence, a fact that gave her a chance to see exactly how many of her friends had come to watch. Self Limit apologized to Tommy when her first shot hit the fence, but he only smiled and reassured her that it was all right. Transcendental concentrated on fixing his eyes on the ball, feeling the racket as a part of his body, becoming aware of his footwork and movement, looking for oneness with the exercise at hand. Exaggerate spun his racket, Prettiness picked a winner, Transcendental elected to serve, and Self Limit tried to remember the advice she had just read about receptiveness to the phenomenon of miracles in MIRACLES ARE REAL by I.M. Deluded.

The Match

Game #1

Transcendental serves first, faces the sun, recognizes the saddened state of mind of Sylvia and hits a medium paced serve directly to her forehand. Self Limit is frozen, getting her racket back so late that she fouls her return into the stands. She looks around for a place to hide but there was none. Exaggerate glares at his partner. Prettiness gracefully waltzes to the opposite court and announces the score, 15—Love. Transcendental retrieves the ball and readies himself for the next point.

Exaggerate crouches low for his return of serve, he means business and he's going to establish that fact right away. Transcendental hits his first serve into the net. Exaggerate smiles to himself in the knowledge that he had his opposition right where he wanted them—psyched out. Tommy's second serve goes deep to the backhand, Exaggerate hits late, the ball goes right at Prettiness, who reacts strictly out of self-defense, hits it off the wood and just over the net for a winner. Exaggerate is now exasperated. Prettiness ponders why her racket turned in her hand and remembers the hand cream she put on just before she came. She decides not to wipe it off, however, since she considered it in the best interest of her ladylike image to have the softest hand on the court during the hand shake exercise after the match. 30—Love.

Transcendental serves to Sylvia for the second time, she makes good contact, but Tommy follows to the net and volleys the return to Exaggerate's feet for a winner. Exaggerate finds the whole circumstance hard to comprehend but decides that the luck of the opposition can't possibly last, brushes by the wife without notice and assumes his usual crouched ready position. 40—Love.

Transcendental looks at his partner reassuringly, bounces the ball a couple of times and serves down the middle to Exaggerate's forehand. What a chance to show that cocky fool who the class of this field is. Exaggerate springs into the ball early, hits a topspin drive between 80 and 90 mph right past Prettiness, who is just not fast enough to get her racket on the ball this time. The overspin fails to take effect, however, and the return sails out. Prettiness takes a deep breath and brushes her hair back into place, glances quickly at her reflection in the plate glass to make sure she is indeed all right, then announces the score in her customary fashion. Game. 1—Love. Exaggerate shakes his head, Sylvia says she's sorry, and the players change courts.

Game #2

Exaggerate walks to the line to serve, looks up and sees the sun, deliberates his alternatives, and tells Self Limit to come serve instead. Sylvia still had cement in her elbow but decided that her husband knew best and marched back to do her duty. She took two practice serves, neither made it to the net. Exaggerate announces that they are ready, and they begin. The first point is concluded with a double fault, Exaggerate can't believe it, shakes his head, tells Sylvia to get the damn ball in play and goes to the next court. Love—15.

Self Limit squinted her eyes harder this time and managed to focus on one of the golden spheres that filled her vision. It turned out to be the ball and not the sun, the serve goes in, Transcendental returns short and too high, Exaggerate calls the ball as his own, Sylvia steps back, her eyes focusing only after the point was over. She knew they had won the point, however, as soon as she recognized that devilish grin on her husband's face—that same one she had seen so many times before as he beat her in arm wrestling. Exaggerate announces the score immediately this time. 15—All.

Patricia walks to her prescribed position on the court, remembers what Chris Evert looks like receiving her roses at Wimbledon and prepares to return serve. Sylvia makes good contact for the second time in a row, the serve goes in, Prettiness lobs from her backhand as she always does, Exaggerate calls it and runs to the baseline, loses his visor on the way, mutters to himself as he peers into the sun, but still manages to attempt his "routine" on-the-knees overhead, 120 mph baseline to baseline. His shot goes out and, in his contemplation of the error, he finds it impossible to understand the bad luck he is having, this day of all days! Why?!!! His mind returns to the reality of the present and his body shudders as he hears the soft voice of Prettiness announcing the score. 15—30.

Self Limit picks up the visor that Exaggerate had just dropped, he doesn't notice its absence, and Sylvia can now see the ball. Transcendental received serve by returning cross-court back to Self Limit, who decides she had better force Prettiness to get involved in the game. She does, by hitting down her alley. Prettiness could not get to the ball without lunging, an alternative she immediately rules out as lacking femininity. She bats her eyelashes, esmiles like all Southern diplomats do, and congratulates Self Limit on a fine shot. Exaggerate announces the score in an affirmative tone. 30—All.

Sylvia is so high after passing Prettiness that she plays two more excellent points without even thinking about it, winning the game in a most uncharacteristic show of strength. Her mind had inadvertently slipped into a positive zone, a fact that she would soon realize and consequently lose. Exaggerate tried in vain to rationalize a way to credit himself with their new success but couldn't, since he hadn't even had his racket on the ball. He does announce the score well, however. 1—All.

Game #3

Transcendental chases the balls down for Prettiness as she practices a dozen serves for the gallery. Exaggerate peels off his warm-up and does several jumping jacks in his eager anticipation of getting his hands on that powder puff serve. Self Limit has come off her high of the previous game, again acknowledging her inherent inferiority. Patricia hits her first serve short, too short for Sylvia to handle in a meaningful way, her return hanging in the air long enough for Transcendental to poach and hit it behind her. Prettiness announces the score, beaming all over in recognition of their lead on her service game. 15—Love.

Exaggerate bounces on his toes as he readies himself for the serve. He was in the midst of a fantastic topspin backhand when he was distracted by the sound of a feminine voice in the crowd describing him as a "typical male chauvinist." That's all he needs is some damned liberated woman shooting off her mouth around the home court. He was infuriated and ready to blast Prettiness right off the court with his return when he took a double take at the girl who had made the statement. By inadvertently taking his eyes off the ball to check, he confirmed exactly who it was. Sure enough, long blonde hair, tight yellow tank top and no bra. WOW! — NO BRA! Would you believe an ace for Prettiness? It is obvious to even the most casual observer that Exaggerate now has a conflict of interest to contend with here. But he'll "handle" it. 30—Love.

Sylvia's feathers are ruffled now, her delicate self image definitely threatened by Exaggerate's spontaneous attention to the sideline. Her feelings are hurt, she's flustered and her return rebounds off the fence. Self Limit can't stand the thought of her husband's eyes gazing on those nude photographs in *Playboy*, let alone the real live thing right here at the courts. 40—Love.

Prettiness is basking in glory now. She touches her ear to make sure that her gold hoops are in place, then serves to Exaggerate, who returns nicely to Patricia's backhand corner. He simply hits the ball too hard for her to handle. He loves it and she concedes, a fact that sort of bothers him since, by definition, concession allows no room for struggle. The obvious advantage he was taking of Prettiness with his strength initiates another caustic comment from the braless one. Exaggerate responds with another denuding glance, he unconsciously inhales so that his stomach doesn't stick out, Self Limit takes it all in once more and becomes more inhibited than ever and misses her subsequent return. Game. 2—1, Transcendental leads.

As the players change courts, Exaggerate takes off his warm-up pants and bounces on his toes like a prize fighter between rounds. Prettiness sips Gatorade from a small paper cup; Sylvia finds her sweater and puts it back on to keep that shameless hussy on the sidelines from seeing that her chest is smaller. Transcendental picks up the balls, hands them to Exaggerate, and then leads the procession back to the arena.

Game #4

Exaggerate takes his practice serves quickly. His shoulder is still stiff and a slower warm-up would have certainly been better, but he was anxious to impress the gallery with his superior serving so he started anyway. He connects on his first serve, it is hard, it feels good, but nips the net cord and bounces just past the line for a fault. His milk-toast second serve proves no problem even for Prettiness, who hits the return nicely cross-court. Exaggerate drives it back and surprises Patricia, who is busy holding her perfect follow-through for the photographer. Exaggerate feels that he won that point convincingly, which he did, but his delusionary perspective misrepresents the nature of the problem he still has to solve. He thinks everything is under control, that the match is certainly his own now. 15—Love.

Exaggerate hits an excellent first serve to Transcendental who makes a stabbing lobbed return that floats just over Sylvia's head. Self Limit's initial reaction is to go ahead and take the shot. At the last second she decides that they can't afford the chance, belatedly saying "yours" to Exaggerate, who was traveling full speed ahead to his customary volleying position two feet from the net. Needless to say, the lob goes untouched. Exaggerate doesn't understand and Sylvia says she is sorry in her patented tone. Prettiness understands the score, however, and is not reluctant to announce it. 15—All.

Exaggerate remains befuddled, misses his first serve but does manage to get his second one in. Prettiness responds with a lob over Sylvia's head because it came to her backhand. Exaggerate reverses direction to cover it and manages to get it back with a very nice effort. Unfortunately, Self Limit failed to switch sides when Exaggerate covered the ball behind her. This fatal error allowed Patricia to conclude the point by hitting gently to the obvious opening that he had left. Sylvia apologized timidly, saying that she just didn't know about any "I Formation." 15—30.

Exaggerate is not only frustrated now, but out of breath as well. His fatigue was already beginning to take its toll on his speedy serve. He summons all the strength he can muster for his first serve to Transcendental. His Cannonball serve goes in just as he had hoped, but his charge to the net is slow. Transcendental's return was not a spectacular one but it did present a problem for Exaggerate whose slow footwork left him stranded in "no-man's land." Prettiness eagerly announces the score in her anticipation of a chance to break the "big serve." 15—40.

Exaggerate is disgusted, becomes distraught at what is happening to him, deduces that it had to be Sylvia's fault, then desperately tries to figure out some new strategy to compensate for his wife's inferior showing. His preoccupation with this early turn of events causes him to inadvertantly double fault to Prettiness, the absolute worst thing he had considered doing. This was the straw that broke the camel's back, that reached through exaggeration, that exposed an insecure self, a self that really didn't believe when the chips were down, that succumbed to self-inflicted pressure, that failed because exaggeration as compensation is not real. Game. 3—1, Transcendental and Prettiness lead.

The stage was set early in this match for the outcome. Exaggerate's deluded confidence gradually became desperation as he tried to play the entire court, gambling on the spectacular, trying shots Laver wouldn't consider. Self Limit fell deeper into self-inflicted depression not only because of her innate lack of self-confidence but because of her good husband's utter distraction with the bulging breasts on the sideline. The calculated partner-picking of Prettiness paid off again, allowing for just the opportunity she had hoped for—a free side with success, the chance to bask in the glory of a winner, to exhibit her body to the world, to look good. Transcendental finished the match the same way he began it; within himself, for himself, an amusing way to spend the weekend. Exaggerate and Self Limit experienced another day just like all their others—up and down, rebounding off one extreme to another. Sylvia goes straight home and makes the medicine cabinet her first stop before bed; Exaggerate throws his rackets into the corner of the den, grabs his billfold and heads for the local topless bar; Prettiness checks her lipstick and says good-by to everyone individually, then slips into the closest phone booth to call the results of the match in to the local paper. Transcendental buys himself a Coke, remembers his reading at home and leaves; forgetting, would you believe, all about his glittering trophy.

CHAPTER 2

Smokescreen Realities

The hypothetical mixed doubles match just described in Chapter 1 as the "social smokescreen" is a statement of social reality. Although the personality types it characterizes can rarely be seen in a pure state, the stereotypes attached to them are, nevertheless, very real and a part of us all. Every man, for example, has a little bit of Patricia's vanity within him, simply because our social environment demands it. We all, at one time or another, express the dependency of Self Limit; and for every act of dependence, there is the corresponding shoulder to be leaned on, and that is Exaggerate. The stereotypes are all human characteristics that are bigger than the game the people play. The goal of this recognition is, of course, to mold the development of our self more in the direction of Transcendental. This constructive manipulation of one's own self begins most importantly with a self education of sorts that brings significant insight into the alternatives that stand infinitely at anyone's disposal. Once alternatives are known, choices can then be made away from conditioned social response. Exaggerate, and Prettiness, and Self Limit, did respond socially, by judging their success, and even worth, on external factors established by their environment. Tommy Transcendental was the highest achiever of them all, even within the external standards of their social base. He accomplished his task, however, through a fundamental simplification—a process that allowed him to focus his attention and purpose within, and for, himself. The judgmental factors that surrounded him that day never pierced his cocoon of concentration, and it is that single fact that allowed him to function at a superior level. And that is our goal.

Much of our story centers around a person's ability, or lack of it, to establish a truly positive self image. Much of the thesis of this book deals with the idea that people at play are really people as they are. Thus, by making determined efforts toward self development while playing (i.e., the game of tennis), one can also expand his or her capacity to achieve in everything they do. It is very much a question of life-style, and a contagious philosophy of perfectionism. It is a search for that elusive "best" that we all know is within us, but which always seems to resist release.

The typical tennis club is a very powerful social setting. It is an environment that tends to make players either very serious or very social—both of which inhibit peak performance and interfere with the act of competition. For example, thousands of young married women begin their weekdays at the courts in some kind of organized competition. It is almost exclusively a morning activity and that is interesting, since in that way their tennis activity would seem to be, very literally, the first priority of their day. The calendar of these same women will usually lead them to the Surf Club for lunch, followed by several drinks on the patio of the pool before returning home in time to greet their children from school and their husbands from work. This is a life-style that is very real and it is one that is at the heart of every active program. The social reality of this life-style, however, has implications that extend beyond the obvious, for the peformance of these girls on the courts is far more important that an incidental morning away from the house. The fact is that tennis for most people (and these "tennis ladies" are just an example), is the most real standard bearer of personal achievement that they have. Its function is as an evaluative device, and it is from this reference that they attain much of their personal self image within the social context. In this way, the game becomes the great equalizer—a leveler that negates everything from inherited wealth, business position, salary, and even blue blood. It reduces life to a duel of sorts between two men on equal footing to see who is best. The objective nature of the score, and the fact that one person's name goes into the win column and the other's into the loser column, makes every player face a very objective truth about himself. Sometimes this truth is so real that it is hard to accept, and it is from this group that we get the great rationalizers—the excuse makers that approach their life the same way a gambler would who seems always to get barely nosed out at the finish. It is the proverbial phenomenon of "almost" or "what if." Even casual observation makes it clear that in some very real social ways . . . you are your tennis game. The great cliché is that "it is only a game," but the social reality of it all would seem to insist otherwise. The fact is that it is much more than that.

It is not unusual to see the game, and the externality of being labeled either a winner or loser, take forms that more than border on the unethical or dishonest. Close calls are signaled out, that causes a reciprocal paranoia to develop from both sides of the net. To compete—and to win—is a contemporary ideal that has been all but institutionalized. It is our way—"free enterprise," "survival of the fittest," "what you earn is what you get." The evolution of this phenomenon and its reflection in the game is interesting. The intensity for success that obsessed Nixon in his politics is not unlike the unrealistic drive some people display on the court under the contemporary philosophy that sanctions the concept of "Do anything to win." The large sums of money that are in the game now has violated some of its former purity. Many a child is contaminated by undue pressure from parents that read financial bliss into their future from a few uninhibited wins. The degree of vicarious association that is expressed by the typical "tennis parent" can border on the unbelievable. Picture, for example, the very aggressive car dealer (plaid sport jacket, white shoes, and shiny car) who shuttles his daughter to and from every tournament. If only from the habit of getting everything he can from every deal he makes, it is that same indoctrination that inevitably shows up as his child begins to compete. His daughter becomes all but another car deal (for she is an extension of himself), and losing is something that he is just not used to . . . after all that is bad business, and one has to be tough to succeed in business these days. It is within this not so distorted context that so many children learn the wrong definition of "toughness." Paranoia reinforces more paranoia, and yes, why not . . . "when in doubt, call it out."

A bit of historical perspective is not unuseful here since morality, and value, and the way people approach their lives (and consequently the game) change and evolve through the years. Don Budge, for example, lived and played the game in an era of noble American idealism. Patriotism, and sportsmanship, and the Davis Cup were virtuous then. But, today we are in the middle of a time of brash competitiveness. The American way is now typified by the likes of Jimmy Connors and his entourage of managers and handlers. It is now the norm to be identified as another of "Peck's Bad Boys." Much of the old ethic of "how to play the game" is gone, for it is no longer so much how you play but whether you win or not that counts. This one obsession . . . TO WIN . . . is the creator of an almost incalculable environment of external pressure. And it is from this extract that the unruly factors of external judgment arise. It is an oppressive environment that ambiguously demands success on one hand but inhibits it on the other. Transcendence of these externals is a necessity if one is to succeed within this frame of reference, and that is what this book is about. The "how to" of this process is revealed in our next discussion: Part II, Threading the Needle.

Part II

THREADING THE NEEDLE

CHAPTER 3

The Self-Limiting Self

The most persistent obstacle that confronts any tennis player as he learns the game, and eventually as he competes, is himself. There are thousands of potential champions who pick up rackets every day. Yet, very few reach their physical potential because they fail to recognize the fundamental dependence of the physical performance on the mind. There is no higher virtue than self-control and tennis provides a challenge in control to both the body and the mind.

The "self-limiting self" is a universal trait of the human condition. Doubt is relative and even though we have all felt it, every individual feels it at levels and in circumstances peculiar to himself. World class competitors feel the same anxiety that the Sunday hack does. Both feel it when they question themselves by wanting the win too much or by feeling they have reached what they unconsciously consider a personal performance peak. Most often these judgments are made in relation to external goals: the relative value of the match, the size of the tournament, the amount of the purse, or the reputation of the opposition. It is by responding to external goals that one unconsciously creates pressure that ultimately inhibits his performance. The mature player—the master of the inner game—focuses the challenge within himself. Beating the world is an assignment too big for any one man, but developing a personal skill level to the maximum and reaching a potential that may in fact earn a Number One world ranking is something different indeed. The focus and challenge must always be within the individual.

There are several essential ingredients that one must recognize as one seeks to learn or compete up to his true potential:

1. You must really want to learn or win;
2. You must be willing to do something significant about it (i.e., work);
3. You must believe that you can do it.

And there is a very real difference between acknowledging that the task in question can be done, and believing that you in particular can do it.

On Learning

With the game of tennis growing at the present rate, every teaching professional encounters a large number of beginning players. The main thing that I try to impart to my students during this early stage of development is the belief that he or she really can do it. Every beginner is reluctant at the start. Most often he or she was turned on to the game after watching the effortless execution of televised matches or by a friend who already knew how to play. But no matter how they got the message, they inevitably face starting somewhere below that initial point of reference. Beginners must begin. This initial period of frustration no doubt results from the instant everything philosophy that seems to be prevalent today—often wanting more than the body can possibly cope with. The "I wonder if I can—I can't" crisis can be beat, however, once the student accepts the notion that the mind must first understand the problem, that it must then work to solve it, and that both processes take time. If it were any other way, there would be no challenge to the game.

Once the initial stage of development is passed, once the student decides that it feels good to hit the ball in the center of the racket, he must be educated to the real potential of his body. It is a marvelous machine, to say the very least. For example, I've seen many women begin playing with the preconceived notion that they just can't run or that ladies just don't serve well. The fact is that we can all do much more than we think we can. Women can run if they want to, they can serve and they can volley, too. It is possible for the clever pro to gently bait these students into performing these tasks, after which he will no doubt hear in an astonished tone: "I didn't know I could do that!" I believe that, if it's necessary, the pro should even create success at this point. Once the student is enlightened to the fact that he can do just one thing that he hadn't previously thought possible, the door is open. He or she will then be caught up in the intangible search for truth that infects us

Children are the best learners in the world

all. As Jonathan Livingston Seagull attempted to sail higher, so will the inspired tennis player reach for perfection. I like to see my students gutting it out, giving more than 100 percent. When I see this, I know that they have abandoned any preconceived notions concerning their physical limitations. I know that they are assuming nothing, that they are seeking whatever their innate potential might be, that the classic problem of overcoming inhibition in order to reach par, has been beaten.

Children enter the learning experience spontaneously. In every way they are growing, in bloom. Every day they reach new heights, have new experiences, do things they hadn't done the day before. This refreshing optimism of youth is what I always hope to instill into my students—the belief that they don't know what they can or can't do until they try, that the human potential is boundless, that they can play the game and that they should intend to experience the rewards that it brings.

Childlikeness in Competition

Childlikeness in competition is a significant idea and, in essence, it simply implies spontaneity, a transcending consciousness. It requires completely freeing oneself of the external obstacles that some people call motivations or goals—winning trophies, money and rankings—and becoming completely at one with experience at hand. At this level of the game, hitting the ball, feeling the ball on the racket, becomes a flowing ever-changing art form. You become an artist, a creator, a master planner of the ball, its placement—challenging your body and meeting it from within. The body and mind become one, acting in unison.

It is ironic how childlikeness at this level requires the maturity of experience and age. Like a U-shaped curve, we all begin our lives at the highest and most pure level of consciousness for learning and achieving. When we learn to walk and talk, we are not instructed to move our tongues and lips in ten thousand variations and we are never told to move our left foot precisely three and one-quarter inches in front of the right for our first step. Through the conscious efforts of the adult world to educate, we soon become desensitized to the oneness of the mind and body, of experience. In general, we face the prospect of becoming segregated. We are conditioned to think too much. The downward trend of the curve is most prominently observed in junior level tennis because as a general rule they are the victims of over coaching and over protective parents seeking the vicarious experience of their children on the courts. Naturally, the only thing the men at the office or the women across the

of thinking is what is really
were based on the fundame ... ...ce was
bad, is bad, is going to cont ... player in ques-
tion was in fact going to lo... the match before he actually had. Also
worth noting is the inevitabl... inforcement that such a prominent display of anxiety gives the oppo... . Imagine the comfort of knowing that
you were working on the man... n one side of the court while he was
working on himself on the other... n say from personal experience that
this is indeed a margin for error I enjoy. One can feel comfortable
trying the most spectacular shots ... ause the chances are good that a
second chance will certainly be there... imilarly, but on the other side of
the coin, a player can very sadistically... use himself by just keeping the
ball in play, watching his opposition or tematically going about the
business of beating himself. It is intere... for the careful observer to
note the muscle tone tighten; the facial n- ressions of pain, question,
doubt, and frustration. The commentary the ccompanies this behavior
is often amusing and runs the gamut from ame-calling to personal
dialogue between the player and himself—pleas ng, begging, cursing. A
case in point might well be that an error was ade on the backhand.
Within the exaggerated context, however, a sing rror can be projected
to the backhand as a whole being bad—that it's vays been bad, that
it's a damn bad day, "Hell, I'll never hit a good ckhand," "Please
don't hit it to my backhand," "Oh, no. It's coming my backhand, I
know I'm going to miss, I missed."

Thus we have the logic of exaggerated emotion on the urt—the self-
limiting self in action. The smart player, the controlled p ver, is one
who masters his emotional responses and operates from within playing
each shot one at a time without generalization, without assum. the
past to be a prediction. Once the shot is made or missed it becomes
history. The mature player's goal is to become the complete master of
the present.

Tennis:

table are
ed, black
lity of th

nto the fence or

CHAPTER 4

Exaggeration and Confidence

The self-limiting self is one extreme of man's emotional makeup. On the other side of the fence, in an opposite extreme, is the exaggerated self, the deluded—and deluding—self, the unrealistic self, the self that looms bigger than life. The interesting thing about this condition is that most of the exaggerated selves we observe in our daily lives represent compensation for an otherwise insecure self. Be that as it may, some men really do believe in their greatness and men really are great. World class champions—the big-timers—characterize this condition. They have to believe in themselves in an exaggerated way in order to remain steadfast under the competition and pressure from a constant onslaught of opposition—psychological and physical, real and imagined. The All American Athlete, the humble champion, the modest winner—they are myths for appearance sake because it's a pleasant image. It is not a practical way for a man to relate to himself and achieve at this level. The bigger the scale, the larger the win, the more illusive the goal, and the more exaggerated belief an individual must have in himself. There is simply no room in the championship performance for modest realism. The acknowledgment of any possibility other than oneself adorned in victorious glory becomes an expression of doubt; and any doubt at all loses in close competition where the relative skill level of the contestants is about the same. The winner under these circumstances is always the man who wants it the most, believes in himself more. Many people imitate the exaggerated selves of acknowledged champions, living a fantasy of vicarious experience.

The real winner comes about his realization without conscious effort. For him it is a conscious rational decision. He believes he is a superior human being, a higher form, godliness embodied, an Atlas. A realist, for example, might acknowledge himself as having unusual talent but would also recognize the fact that others possess it in similar degrees, and that any of these otherwise equal specimens could—and would—beat each other on a given day. The exaggerated self, however, will never recognize such a fact. His rationalization would no doubt be that he was unquestionably the most outstanding talent anywhere, that on occasions that he did lose, luck was against him, he didn't feel well, the linesmen were bad, his favorite racket was broken, the wind was blowing, or his opponent was either blind or deliberately called those line shots out. The losing explanation will always imply that unusual circumstances were at work, that something extremely abnormal happened to keep his superior talent from prevailing.

Examples of the Real Thing

The most outstanding example of the exaggerated self at work, the most profound demonstration of the power of positive thinking, of really believing in spite of the world that you were the very best, is Muhammad Ali. The world had never seen anyone like Cassius Clay when he met Sonny Liston on February 24, 1964 for the heavyweight championship of the world.

Clay, only twenty-one at the time, had won nineteen professional bouts but had distinguished himself more prominently as the "Louisville Lip" because of his apparently exaggerated public claims of greatness. Sonny Liston, a brute of a man, had only recently twice disposed of Floyd Patterson, both times in the first round. Liston was considered all but invincible. By the day of the fight, when all the rhetoric for the benefit of the press was supposed to be over, Cassius Clay went "crazy." With Sugar Ray Robinson at his side at the weigh in, Clay shouted, "You tell Sonny I'm here with Sugar Ray—Liston is flat-footed but me and Sugar Ray are pretty dancers. Round eight to prove I'm great, float like a butterfly, sting like a bee." Clay's pulse rate, normaly fifty-four beats a minute, shot up—at the weigh in—to 120. Clearly the emotional side of Cassius Clay was out of control; his exaggerated self out of proportion beyond all rational explanation, complete and total obses-

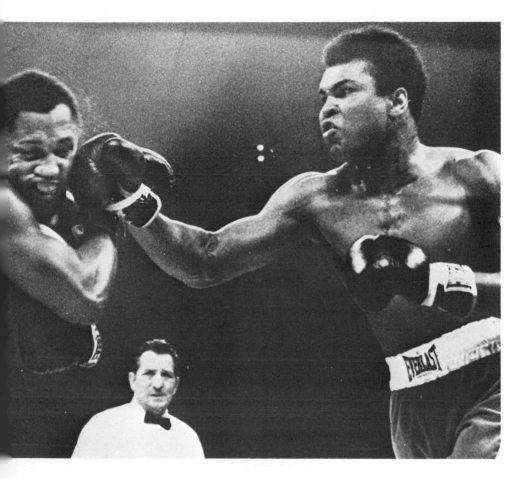

Muhammad Ali said he was the greatest and he was

sion with himself and the task at hand. The world was aghast when Clay pretty-danced his way to victory in the seventh round, becoming the new heavyweight champion of the world. The significant thing about the Clay phenomenon, however, is not that he won the title, but rather how he accepted and beat the ensuing tragedy of his career, the eventual stripping of the title because of his refusal to dance to the drums of the draft, his refusal, for religious reasons, to let the Selective Service make him a soldier. Muhammad Ali, his new Muslim name, was denied the best years of his career while in and out of court over his religious convictions. But on October 26, 1970, after three and a half years of inactivity, he began one of the most famous comebacks in sports history by beating Jerry Quarry in Atlanta in a technical knockout. Everything pointed toward a title bout with the current champion Joe Frazier, and on March 8, 1971, Ali's exaggerated ego faced the supreme test. He lost a fifteen round decision in one of the greatest fights of all time. What would happen to this man who had never lost? His self image did not change. He lost another fight along his comeback trail to Ken Norton, a fight, and defeat, that left many skeptics proclaiming Ali's efforts an exercise in futility, that the Ali era was over, that the "sting" was gone, that his body was through. Ali did not accept that premise. Instead, he worked and trained and eventually won his title back three years later by defeating the vital and undefeated champion, George Foreman. Muhammad Ali believed in himself. He believed when the world thought he was too young and inexperienced to fight Sonny Liston. He believed when the world thought he was too old to fight George Foreman. The saga of Muhammad Ali should stand as an example to us all of what desire and self commitment can do. He said he was the greatest, he believed he was the greatest. Indeed, he proved he was the greatest. Jose Torres sums up the story well:

> He was American in a way few others were American because in him there was always the possibility of tragedy. He was a romantic, a man that believed in possibilities; if you believed hard enough you could become the Olympic champion, the world's heavyweight champ, you could have expensive houses, the Cadillacs, and you could do it without compromising, without being damaged, without being hurt. Muhammad Ali—black prince.

There are notable examples of exaggerated egos in other sports as

well. Walt Frazier, the dynamic guard for the New York Knicker-
bockers has made several interesting statements that reveal much about
his self image. In response to the question of whether any athlete is
worth $300,000 a year, he says simply "I think I'm worth more than
that. I don't think they could ever pay me enough." Commenting on a
statement he had previously made about his being the most complete
ball player in basketball he replied, "Well, I'm the best all around
guard, I can do everything." But even more revealing that any other
statement: "I don't need guys telling me how great I am—I can tell myself and believe it."

Muhammad Ali and Walt Frazer make extreme statements, both live
up to them, but even they don't have quite the sense of grandeur that
possesses motorcycle stuntman Evel Knevil. This is a man whose ego is
literally bigger than life. He not only believes he is the greatest, he bets
his life on it every time he competes. In the nature of his feat, he necessarily competes against himself, a fact that destines him to lose eventually. Every man has an innate potential, a limit, and Evel Knevil will
certainly find his sooner or later. There is no sense of reality for this
man, never a sense of the rational or of fear. He will eventually try to
hurtle one Mack truck too many or soar over one canyon too wide. For
the present time, of course, he lives as the best, a winner in the most
glamorous way, an exaggerated ego in success. His is the saddest saga of
them all, however, for his delusion, all of his victories, will eventually
cost him his life. He states his philosophy as follows:

> I think it's better to risk my life and be a has-been than to
> have never been at all. Even though crippled and busted in
> half, it's better to have taken a chance to win a victory or suf-
> fer a defeat than to live like others do who will never know
> victory or defeat because they haven't had the guts to try
> either.
>
> —*Evel Knevil*

Tennis players are no different than any other athletes in this respect.
In many ways, in fact, they are more individualistic and more callous,
since the nature of the sport is by definition individual head on head
competition. The security of teammates for rationalization or escape is
an unknown luxury. No one compensates for you during the failing performance. Whatever happens on the court is to the credit or discredit of
the individual, good or bad, each man's fate his personal responsibility.

Many people call Jimmy Connors "cocky," a spoiled brat, a prima donna. In spite of it all, however, even his most severe critic must admit that he dominated the game in 1974. His arrogance rebuffs many, crowds come to see him lose rather than win. Ali won his title back in spite of his critics, the American establishment and the United States Army. Evel Knevil does his thing even if he has to buy his own canyon to do it. And Jimmy Connors wins the 1974 Forest Hills final over Ken Rosewall with the loss of only two games in three sets. Connors is arrogant, he is cocky and he is rich. He is a hardened match-tough competitor who is self-centered, a perfectionist and a champion's champion to others. He is a winner in a most dynamic way.

CHAPTER 5

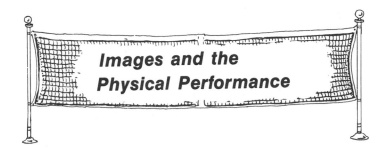

Images and the Physical Performance

The state of a person's mind during the physical performance is an interesting and very difficult problem to understand. To begin with, everything we do in life is some kind of physical performance. We do all kinds of things during our daily lives and our minds operate from just as many different levels. For example, our heart beat is a physical performance but our mind does not direct it. We learn to walk, an act we eventually learn to do without conscious effort. It is interesting to ponder the thought patterns of the child as he learns to walk because of the fact that walking occurs before he comprehends language. Thus, whatever the thought patterns are they are on a level of consciousness beyond that of language. There can be no conscious instructions, no left foot then right. There is no duality of the self—the child is truly at one with the experience. There is an interesting and spontaneous state at work here, one worth considering when one really thinks about the complexity of the problem that was solved that day we first decided it was time to walk. The relevance of this level of consciousness to tennis is very obvious because of the difficulty of the problem that was solved and the comparative simplicity of the task we are concerned with—playing tennis effectively.

It is my opinion that learning and performing at this level requires the use of images, mental images formed without the aid of language but instead through the use of our basic senses of sight, sound and feel. The child was aware before he walked that those around him were standing

43

and moving from an erect position. During the time that elapsed where his body matured to the point where he had a walking capability, the child unconsciously forms images of what it would be like to walk. He had watched, learned, imagined, and then acted in imitation. The formation of images at this level requires anticipation, picturing the act in a time sequence slightly ahead of the present. I have told students to pretend that they are viewing a video tape that is taking place five seconds in the future, picturing themselves making the shot they are about to try, experiencing themselves in the act of success. This is a significant thought because it amounts to positive thinking in the purest form. It simply leaves no room for doubt. It is easy to understand when one considers exactly what anxiety and lack of confidence on the court is. It is a circumstance that takes place in exactly the same way, except in reverse; the mind fearing and doubting an upcoming shot just previous to execution, forming negative mental images rather than positive ones. Our goal, of course, must be to use the formation of images in a positive way—seeing ourselves and not just the shot, executing the shot successfully.

Musicians are good at reaching this transcendent level of consciousness. They call it "feeling their music." My enlightenment to this fact occurred very spontaneously one night as I sat beside an excellent banjo player. I was absolutely obsessed with the level of consciousness that he was working from as his fingers raced across the strings with his right hand, his left playing chords and his voice singing words. A very interesting physical feat was obviously at work here. Where was his mind? For sure he wasn't thinking about the execution of specific physical acts. It was not a segmented performance. It was a total experience; voice, hands, and mind all working as one. He was feeling, feeling the musical act as a whole, slightly ahead of its actual execution—musical images, hearing, listening, imagining, indeed feeling the music. The significant thing about this idea of musical images is how it portrays how the mind is capable of handling the entirety of an experience at a transcendental level.

This is precisely what the tennis player should seek to achieve; a level of consciousness that encompasses the entire performance, one that sees a man through a whole match in a positive way. This, of course, is not easy. For example, it is a common pitfall to "let up" after building a substantial lead. An effective level of awareness was reached, it was working to the point of outclassing your opponent, you realize it by recognizing the score and other external factors, and it is lost. The opponent is then given new life, the score becomes close, you try in desperation to will yourself back into the transcendent state but can't, you become frustrated and your effectiveness diminishes. The luxury of skipping to and from this level does not exist because the unconscious cannot be consciously manipulated.

I've experienced this relationship between positive thinking and the transcendent consciousness often while competing in target matches with pistols. Extreme concentration is necessary here simply to avoid the distraction of nine other .45 caliber shots going off simultaneously in rapid fire competition. When the level is reached here, one hears nothing, you are aware of the essence of the gun as an extension of your body and nothing else. The competitive act happens too fast to deliberate winning and losing. Everyone competes simultaneously. The essence of the competition is necessarily against oneself and that is exactly what tennis players need more of. They need less personal debate over the score and winning, and how they think they are doing. There needs to be much more emphasis within the individual, against one's self, against a person's own potential—a factor that is always unknown and always slightly ahead of your present state.

During the actual physical act of firing, the gun and even the bullet become a projection of yourself, an extension of your body. There are times that this oneness with the experience is so great that you simply feel that you are willing the bullets into the bull's-eye, and in a sense you are. The fact is that the strength of the positive image merely left no room for negative alternatives for the body or self-limiting self to consider. There can be total strength in positive thinking through images. It is difficult to understand; indeed, attempts to make it rational spell its certain downfall. The essence of this dilemma in this experience is, fundamentally, that the mind and its unusual control of the body are at a level beyond what mortals can ever hope to understand or explain through science or logic. The powers of the mind are complex but, more significantly, they are a gift—one that we should acknowledge and not question.

Projecting the transcendent state from music to shooting to tennis is certainly possible. It is difficult, however, because external temptation has more time to thrive in tennis. There is more time to think. There is more opportunity for the development of negative thought patterns and they have more of a chance to work their undoing magic, more time for the duality of the self to debate success and failure, winning and losing, good play and bad.

Direct parallels can be drawn between target shooting on the range and serving for, unlike all other shots in tennis, the player is in complete control from beginning to end, never responding to the initiatives of another. Although every shot in tennis is a target exercise of sorts, serving is by far the most obvious. The externality of the opponent is irrelevant for, by definition, he must respond to you, at your will not his. All of the significant elements of the serving performance are within you. You simply pick a spot in the service court, focus your eyes on it, relax your body, imagine the upcoming serve hitting the desired spot, then glide rhythmically into a duplication of the feeling that you have just vicariously experienced through images. A truly transcendental image will feel so complete, so real, that the physical senses feel the experience, feel the image, as they do in actual execution. Indeed, it is possible that one might debate which experience is the most real.

There is a relevant projection of the serving mentality to all other shots on the court, it is simply more difficult, a later stage in one's transcendental development. The formation of images is, of course, the key. For example, I remember spending hours in front of a mirror as a child, imitating photographs of Rosewall's swing. I was, without knowing its significance, forming personal images of myself with Rosewall's swing, projecting Rosewall's appearance on the court to myself. It proved to be an effective learning technique. Images train the body and images train the mind. Complete image formation implies believing, thinking positive, seeing one's personal capabilities in success. Success, however, does not happen accidently—an investment is made, you work for it, it is a condition that is earned.

CHAPTER 6

Goal Orientation

Why do most people play tennis? What do I personally attempt to instill my students to seek from the game? These are two different questions with two entirely different answers. In dealing with the first, there are probably as many specific answers as there are individuals playing the game. Even so, there are several general types of players who are lured to the courts for similar reasons, a short discussion of each being appropriate to understand and more fully contrast the inner and external goal orientation of tennis players.

Because we are living in the midst of what many are calling the "tennis boom," it is not uncommon to see people playing the game simply because it is part of the current public fascination. Tennis became suddenly visible, matches were televised, tennis commercials and ads became popular; in short it became fashionable to be a tennis player. Clothes designers picked up the scent early, offering an endless variety of "pretty things to wear." Women love this. There are women's leagues and teams everywhere now, and while many of the ladies do have a genuine competitive streak in them, many are there in the same way women flock to the beaches in the summertime—participation in a socially accepted form of exhibitionism. The interesting thing to me about this whole phenomenon is that while the plumage of women may have been the underlying lure that brought them to the game, these "beautiful people" almost inevitably end up doing themselves a lot of good. They become more aware of the fundamentally physical nature of their bodies and it assumes a meaning and feel beyond the detached way it might have previously appeared in the mirror. They become fit, they become healthier, their bodies trim down and they adorn the courts in a naturally beautiful and wholesome way; and this is the "paradox of prettiness" in tennis.

Women are not the only ones that show up at the courts for other than the obvious reasons. Men are just as susceptible to vanity as are women. But, the first and most characteristic role that men adopt on the court is one of superiority—masculinity embodied, the big game, the hundred mile an hour slam that dusts the line. Husbands like nothing better than the opportunity to keep their wives in line by beating them in tennis. Needless to say, those who aren't damned sure of the outcome don't bother. Imagine the humiliation at the breakfast table, the resulting insecurity, the threat to masculine dominance, feminine superiority— DIVORCE? Perhaps that is a bit extreme, but the pressures are there nevertheless. Think of the public interest that was stirred up by Bobby Riggs in his challenge to Margaret Court on Mother's Day. The feminists did get a measure of revenge, however, when Billie Jean King beat the Sugar Daddy in the "Battle of the Sexes" at the Astrodome. The whole affair was good for the game, good for women and women's tennis. It was all needed and probably deserved. The only footnote that I might add is that their entire case was blown equally out of proportion by no more than a clever old man who pulled off one the biggest hustles in years by fanning the flames of feminine insecurity.

The fact that tennis is a competitive sport brings another interesting dimension of the human spirit to light. Some people, for different reasons, love to compete. There are some who compete because they are blessed with a specific talent that allows them to assert themselves over others. This is not an uncharacteristic trait in people. We all seek dominance at some time doing something and, for those with a talent for the game, tennis becomes a legitimate outlet. But winning for winning's sake alone is not the only lure to competition anymore. There are substantial material gains to be had if one gets good enough. Young players can look forward to college scholarships and expense paid travel, prize money tournaments and public recognition. Thus, the designation "winner" is sought after in a myriad of degrees but for two fundamental reasons. Some seek self exaltation, the personal gratification of being able to directly assert themselves over another through headlines and shiny silverware. Others are lured by the more materialistic goals that revolve around money and opportunity. But in spite of which one of these characteristics dominates the motivations of two people as they face each other across the net, the facts and the results are almost always the same—two people challenging themselves and another after hours of practice and thought for one reason—TO WIN.

Tennis is also a game with a potential social function. Many young people, for example, find that it can be a convenient means for dating. Doubles and mixed doubles are always enjoyable in this way, where having fun is the primary function and winning second. Age and ability have nothing to do with tennis here; rather, people are the essential ingredient. A person can go most anywhere and see the game fulfilling this function, people trying to work together, coordinating separate efforts to form an integrated result. The idea of a doubles team is particularly catching here in the United States where the public is so definitely team oriented—football teams, basketball teams, baseball teams, tennis teams! Would you believe World Team Tennis? Certainly. We are a gregarious species and find it particularly challenging and enjoyable to work and play together.

There are a great many players today who profess to play the game basically for the exercise. Our sophisticated technology continues to do more work for us, a fact that leaves modern man not only with more time on his hands but with an increased responsibility to use it constructively. People are deciding that they had better put down the beer cans and turn off the TV. I think there has always been a rather well-accepted prejudice against the education of the physical, the main source of rationalization being the liberal arts inspired stigma of anti-intellectualism. The irony is complete now, however, as one observes the increasing numbers of professional people (doctors, lawyers, business executives, teachers) picking up rackets in their spare time. It is interesting because what had formerly been one of the most aloof segments of our society is now experiencing the belated recognition that they had better stay in shape if they expect their minds to function up to their potential. Tennis, in particular, provides a physical challenge to the body and a distinct mental exercise for those who choose to use it as such and think on the court. Physical fitness is certainly a relevant goal and tennis is a legitimate answer for those whose desire it is to maintain their good health.

Another sad but true reason that some people play is to please others. It is not an uncommon occurrence among young players who, for one reason or another, find it necessary to please their parents at their expense. Family tradition or vicarious parental experience, the rationalization is for the most part irrelevant. The significant fact is that the pressure is real and that the personal goal orientation of the child is consequently negative.

On the other extreme, of course, are those players who really play the game for fun. Hitting the ball, running, playing, and interacting in a wholesome way with another of common interest is a stimulating combination to many people. It is an activity that is enjoyable, relaxing, something that you look forward to doing in your spare time. It is a challenge on one hand and a good time on the other. The fact is that we should all play less seriously and more for the enjoyment of active participation. Playing for fun should be a fundamental priority for each of us.

As a Microcosm of Life

I have lived tennis as a way of life. It was always an obsession that headed all other priorities. Indeed, it shaped them, and it is because of this that I feel that any true message about tennis is also one about life; very simply a lesson in excellence with the game serving as a medium.

I have learned about people on the tennis court because there are no social curtains there. In the teaching experience I am an observer, almost an intruder, in an experience between the student and his self. The question of talent is not a significant one to me, the important variable instead being how seriously the individual takes his own personal development. In its essence, I would have to say that the most fundamental aspect of my philosophy of learning centers around the overused cliché about doing something right or not doing it at all. I don't believe that there is any room in life or on the courts for half efforts, for less than total personal commitment to one's self. I don't believe the idea of compromise. For example, I have had a number of students over sixty-five who have been an inspiration to everything I have done. Their enthusiasm, indeed their optimism of youth, their willingness to reach for personal limitations, has been beautiful. These people have known about living. They had not receded into the rocking chair. They were searching and striving in the most committed positive way for personal fulfillment. One of the rules that I set on my court is the absence of clocks, the elimination of time as an agent of control. The fundamental premise behind that thought is that the playing experience should always be done at 100 percent, that the goal should not be to pace one's self to last the duration of the hour, but that we should go as hard as we can during the playing process, that when limits are reached we rest, and talk, and then do it again. There can be no compromising the process. My goal is to act as an agent of my student's conscience, pushing him just a little farther than his conscious self would otherwise consider doing. I hit the ball just a little too far away, close enough that he has to try, far enough that half efforts fail. I search for limits and only insist that honest limits are reached. I share the fulfillment of my grey-haired ladies because we both know that they gave everything they had, that their commitment was total, that their experience was satisfying, and that they were successful in the most real way.

I have a real hang-up about wasted talent and how that and isolated match wins are so readily rewarded. Success and reward, for me, cannot be so heavily weighted to favor external goals. These are priorities that have to be set from within, with the individual himself being the only one to ever really know real and honest and full commitment was made. The whole learning process, indeed every experience on the court or elsewhere, should be considered a personal challenge. The individual that lives to make life a test, that lives to challenge himself, will not fail. I instill this idea of sacrifice into many of my students through running, because it is work to push your body several miles, because it hurts, because the lesson is to learn to do something that you dislike, because it increases your personal investment, because you become more aware of your body, its limits, its potential. Of course, it tests your body and you will certainly get stronger, but the significant import of running is distinctly mental, to push yourself one step farther, to find a personal limit and then increase it. These are the individuals that concentrate more, try harder, hit the last ball in the court. Concentration and effort are synonymous terms, for it takes considerable effort to endure pain, to overcome the easy out, not to quit, to succeed. A man who lived this idea as much as any was the famous acrobat and top mounter, master of the infinitely difficult one finger stand, Whitey Caron. He described fighting a "miss," fighting failure, in a recent letter:

> You took it of your own volition, now . . . stay there! Fight it. I would actually pull free of the miss talking to myself this way . . . fighting an unseen opponent (with the intent to win of course); and I would often push without the aid of the left hand out of the miss and into a hit! With the hardest part accomplished, I simply said again . . . there you bastard, if you did that you can do more! Then into a sleeper and the

maintenance of it for such a period that only intense upside down laughter would cause me to come down and do more over and over and over, until I was sick of it, as I knew practice made perfect. Never quitting, never giving up.

And on pride and concentration, he said:

The lock and the freeze, the 'finito' that was coasting. Sheer joy. The vision of my seeing only my straight arm perpendicular to his skull, unable to see him under me except for his massive chest sticking out, the line up so clean that I could not see his feet; my own mind on the thought Stay, Stay, Stay. I would focus on the back of my hand, feel the exertion of my own muscles, the strain (yes, and pain) which I found exhilarating because I knew that I was doing something unusual; certainly not the norm, and by far in excess of what other top mounters were doing.

Concentration is discipline—mental discipline. Achievers make large personal investments, the tortoise that outran the hare. One of the saddest ironies of all, in tennis or otherwise, is that those who are blessed with talent often get away with a minimal personal investment and still succeed. It is true that the success they find is an artificial one, one that loses in the long run, but it is nevertheless an external reward that influences the talented to bask in their glory, one that misrepresents the nature of true success. The arrogance of talent without commitment has to be one of the greatest of injustices. These child prodigies often come back, their patented line being . . . "Yes, but I could have done it." The sad thing is that they didn't make it because they took it for granted, because they weren't willing to make the investment, because achievement requires guts. Even sadder than the comparatively insignificant failure to reach a personal high in tennis, is the fact that half efforts become a way of life. I don't buy the idea of spending yourself in degrees. The achiever doesn't tolerate less than a full effort from himself in anything. It boils down to the question of pride, being able to live with yourself, knowing that you did your best, that your goal was a personal one, of personal achievement, for personal satisfaction. Real winners try harder. The champion is a mixture of talent and commitment, desire and effort. But, the world champion and my gray-haired beginners walk a common ground. They know that worthwhile things don't

Whitey Caron -- famous acrobat and top mounter

come easy, that external rewards are nice, but that real satisfaction comes from within.

In a story about the world's most famous gull, Jonathan Livingston Seagull, Richard Bach describes some important things about life and living. As a young gull Jonathan was obsessed with flying and with learning. He said, "I don't mind being bone and feathers, mom. I just want to know what I can do in the air and what I can't, that's all. I just want to know." After that day he went buzzing through the Breakfast Flock at the unheard of speed of 212 miles an hour, he was banished as a heretic. Elder Gull said to him, ". . . one day Jonathan Livingston Seagull, you shall learn that irresponsibility does not pay. Life is the unknown and the unknowable, except that we are put into this world to eat, to stay alive as long as we possibly can."

Seagulls never spoke back to the Council Flock but Jonathan raised his voice and said, ". . . who is more responsible than a gull who finds and follows a meaning, a higher purpose for life. For a thousand years we have scrabbled for fish heads, but now we have a reason to live—to learn, to discover, to be free."

Jonathan continued his search for meaning all his life. He learned after death that heaven was not a place but that heaven was perfection. The Elder said to him, "You will begin to touch heaven, Jonathan, in the moment that you touch perfect speed. And that isn't flying a thousand miles an hour, or a million, or at the speed of light. Because any number is a limit, and perfection doesn't have limits. Perfect speed, my son, is being there."

Expounding on the idea that speed in flying was merely the tangible aspect of a more abstract goal, he said further, ". . . the gulls who scorn perfection for the sake of travel go nowhere, slowly. Those who put aside travel for the sake of perfection go anywhere, instantly. Remember, Jonathan, heaven isn't a place or a time, because place and time are so very meaningless. Heaven is . . . ."

Jonathan spent his life in pursuit of meaning, of perfection. We all have a bit of Jonathan in us, and we can all find the measure of godliness that he found . . . if we try.

On Losing—Effectively Dealing with the Negative

The phenomenon of losing is universal and it pertains to everything we do, tennis or otherwise. Tennis is simply the medium through which I have chosen to state a number of philosophical anecdotes concerning positivism and positive thinking. The game has been a means to state a theory of living, of life and how to get the most out of it, of commitment and sacrifice and investment.

Like the phenomenon of winning, or of the anxiety of the self-limiting self, losing is also relative. We have all lost and we will all lose again. The thing that separates winners and losers, as we know and recognize them, is how effectively or ineffectively each deals with the negative, how each accepts and relates to the loss, to failure. We have a distinct choice at our disposal. We can defy the losing act, we can reject resignation and do whatever is necessary to change the negative circumstance. Muhammad Ali, for example, lost the "Fight of the Century" in his attempt to reclaim the title he thought was his. He did not, however, accept the negativism of that night, he rejected failure and refused to retire. The inner strength that made that decision possible eventually made him a bigger winner than ever when he defeated George Foreman in 1974. Ali has been a man who has not only possessed a magnificent talent, but he has been one who was willing to work for the things that were important to him. His drive to succeed, to win, have been second to none. Similarly, Margaret Court did not succumb to the accusations of failure that were hurled her way after she lost to Bobby Riggs. She was the best woman player in the world when she entered the match and she proved later that she was still the best when it was over. Both Ali and Court decided to put the past behind them and do something about the future. People cope with failure in an infinitesimal number of ways and at an equal number of different levels. Examples of failing efforts to deal with failure are around us every day because few cope with it positively, few people really do get the most out of themselves, most do in fact limit themselves. *Resignation* is the ultimate disease of the negative and it characterizes people as individuals, people in general, people in classes and even in cultures. Ayn Rand, the famous proponent of individualism, states that her philosophy is . . .

> the concept of man as a heroic being, with his own happiness
> as the moral purpose of his life, with productive achievement
> as his noblest activity, and reason as his only absolute.
> —*Atlas Shrugged, page 1170*

This must be considered a significant thought because, in the heroic being, there is always the possibility of tragedy—but while the potential for tragedy and failure is within us all, productivity and reason offer us an effective way to cope with it. It allows man to find happiness, to find success—to beat failure.

People lose tennis matches for either of two reasons. They lose them because their bodies fail them or because their minds limit them. Bodies do fail at times, even in spite of rigorous training, because we are human and because that simple fact is inherent in all of us as imperfect beings. Failure of this kind is inevitable and it is our job to simply see that it happens as seldom as possible. Our bodies are the tools of our minds and sometimes tools break or need rest.

The more significant failure is the mental one, the negative, the negative, limiting one that we all too often thrust on ourselves. This is the one that really takes discipline to beat. This is the one that always separates the players we see on a world class level from those who "almost made it" that we'll never see. There are quite a few players who can hit a given shot as well as a world class competitor. The dilemma that they faced but failed to cope with was the simple axiom of improvement in anything—and that in essence is the higher the level, the more personal commitment required. Players and all people plateau. They level off on the ladder of success when they stop compensating for failure with increased investment, with more work. No one coasts to the top. People who get there in tennis, anywhere, in any activity, are those who fail like everyone else but who cope with it effectively. In short, they are the ones who do something about their losses, who put the past behind them, declare it a part of history and go about positively affecting their future. These are the winners in every facet of life—and there are real winners everywhere, doing everything, even the most menial tasks. There are also failures on the most grandiose scale. Richard Nixon failed the American people and he failed himself. But the system he tried to foil was made by real winners, and the American public proved that it knew how to win, too—for we have shown that we are a people of conscience. Nixon lost but the system won. It recognized failure and did something about it.

Specific tennis losses must be handled the same way. An objective critique of what happened must be made, conclusions must be drawn, and work must proceed. When losses are incurred, training is increased—longer runs on the beach, pressing and pushing the body further, feeling the pain and not forgetting it, a punishment of sorts, but new limits for sure. More mental discipline, more rote practice to train the fallibility of the body, more commitment to personal goals, yes . . . self sacrifice for the self. That is what this mental game is all about—the truest philosophy of positivism, of people positively affecting their future. Indeed, it would seem that we all do reap what we sow, the universal law of karma being very relevant because we all sow our own seeds of personal success or failure.

Part III

MASTERS OF TRANSCENDANCE

CHAPTER 7

The Rational Exaggeration

The self of rational exaggeration is unusual. The requirements are simply a superior talent and a calculated personal recognition of themselves. These personalities believe in themselves. More importantly, they know themselves, their abilities, their assets and liabilities. It is because of this very rational appraisal of their own game that they always seem to be able to "win at will." These are the selves that don't often fluctuate, that rarely suffer bad losses in big tournaments. They are the personalities that rise to the occasion, that always seem to be up at the right time. They offer themselves the most rational critique of the matches they play. They are pragmatic and they are good at defining their opponents' weaknesses in terms of their own strengths. They know key points and they summon their concentration to meet them. They seem utterly calculating in the heat of high competition. They are relatively emotionless, the kind of self that seems to have ice water running through their veins. They are problem solvers. They are supremely rational, they are a superior talent and they use it almost scientifically for one purpose—to assert themselves, the further themselves, to win. These are the calculated champions. They are John Newcombe and Stan Smith.

John Newcombe

John Newcombe has been a dominant force in tennis since 1965 when he was ranked ninth in the world. By 1967 he was Number One and for the first time recognized as the best player in the world. He slumped in 1968 and 1969 but in 1970 and 1971 he emerged again as the recognized champion of the world. An interim period in John Newcombe's life occurred between 1971 and 1973, the year he regained his untouchable form to win the United States Open at Forest Hills. This period in Newcombe's life is an interesting and very human one because it is a period where he began to acknowledge a realignment of priorities in his life, namely his personal life, his family, and the development of his ranch in Texas, the T BAR M. The style in which he captured the 1973 United States Open is significant to the analysis of John Newcombe's character because it represents the culmination of a rather dramatic comeback. It represents a rational self calculating a comeback potential successfully. It shows a tenacious spirit at work, a confident, utterly cool competitor doing his thing in a most efficient way.

It first became evident that John Newcombe was going to be a force to be contended with at Forest Hills in '73 when he disposed of Andrew Pattison (6-7, 6-1, 7-5, 6-4) after Pattison had just put away the number one seed of the tournament, Ilie Nastase (6-7, 2-6, 6-3, 6-4, 6-4). Pattison played well but Newcombe simply played better. His form continued to hold fast as he handily disposed of Jimmy Connors in the quarters (6-4, 7-6, 7-6). Ken Rosewall had survived the first nine days of the tournament without the loss of a set but he still proved no match for Newcombe in the semis, losing 6-4, 7-6, 6-3. Jan Kodes, whose power off the ground had combined with some precision volleying, found himself in the final with a series of good wins behind him, notable among them being his five set semifinal victory over Stan Smith (7-5, 6-7, 1-6, 6-1, 7-5). Thus, the scene was set for one of the most dramatic finishes Forest Hills fans had seen in years. It was, more specifically, however, a conclusion that stands as a lasting tribute to what John Newcombe is made of. Down two sets to one, his supremely rational being, his ability to respond at peak performance under pressure, his coolness, and his confidence led him in awe-inspiring fashion to a come-from-behind victory, 6-4, 1-6, 4-6, 6-2, 6-3. It was a match that many compare to his comeback victory in the 1971 Wimbledon final over Stan Smith. Richard Evans, of *World Tennis Magazine*, considered that the finest match of Newcombe's career, noting the unusually high level of play from both players, that Jan Kodes also played a most lethal brand of tennis that September day in New York. Reflecting on the Wimbledon victory two years before, Newcombe said . . .

John Newcombe

the one thing you mustn't do is panic. For about an hour, everything that Jan touched turned to gold, but I knew it couldn't last—not if I put pressure on him by getting my second serve deeper and attacking his own serve.

The rational problem solving of John Newcombe was at work again and, indeed, his appraisal proved to have considerable merit. Experience combined with a tenacious will to win, and a championship was won.

John Newcombe followed his prestigious showing at the Open with another series of superlative matches as Australia railroaded the Davis Cup from the United States 5-0 in Cleveland. Many feel that the back of America was broken in the opening match, one where Newcombe defeated Stan Smith in five sets. Two of the game's biggest hitters put their "big games" to work, bludgeoning away at each other and alternating sets before entering the fifth. Smith broke serve in the third game of the final set but Newcombe held on in typical fashion, breaking back in the sixth game to even the score at three-all. The ending was to prove almost anticlimactic after such an even assault, but the fact that Smith double faulted on match point does not erase one important thing: the intangible but profoundly real pressure projected when any man faces John Newcombe across the net when it counts. The final score was 6-1, 3-6, 6-3, 3-6, 6-4 and as they say—"When the going gets tough, the tough get going." John Newcombe once again proved that he was tough when he needed to be.

After Newcombe won Forest Hills over Jan Kodes, he announced in a typically calculated way that he intended to win the World Championship of Tennis. He said that day . . .

> By the end of the W. C. T. tour in May, I want to be accepted as the number one player in the world.

He said that he would win that final shootout in Dallas and he did. His form prevailed, his prophesy was true, and his final opponent that day in May was the young prodigy from Sweden, Bjorn Borg.

The drama of this match began early. Most observers expected the seventeen year old Borg to be a victim of nerves with $50,000 riding on the outcome. Those same people similarly expected to see the experience of Newcombe to steady him from the outset. But as fate and contradiction would have it, this was not to be the case. From the first ball he hit, Borg did his thing, played his game the only way he knew how—100 percent, an all-out onslaught of vicious topspin drives hit with an audacity that was almost beyond belief. Newcombe, on the other hand, began more cautiously, operating on a more real level, aware of the reality of his circumstance and of the significance of the match. He peaked in a deliberate fashion, while Borg's genius relied, by definition, on spontaneity. Newcombe's performance was characterized by conscious control, deliberately plotting a course for himself and adhering to it. A combination of factors played on one another as the audience became mesmerized for that first incredible set—Newcombe's recognition of the time and place he was occupying in history that day, Borg's recklessness, playing completely without abandon, his topspin drives transcending the reality of circumstance. Newcombe's rational problem solving was to take its toll, however. His pressure increased steadily, became relentless, services of thunder and volleys that held an awesome note of finality. The symbolism was there that day and so were the facts—4-6, 6-3, 6-3, 6-2 (Newcombe).

Commenting on this match in his book *Net Results*, Rick Devereux makes several relevant observations. On Newcombe's experience and ability to appraise the situation rationally, he said,

> His greater maturity and experience—Newcombe has thirteen more years of experience than Borg—told him that his own confidence would grow and that Borg could not continue to play so well, 'out of his head' or not. More than any other player in the world today, Newcombe knows that the important matches are not won by playing cooly 'out of your head.' His winners' attitude is universally recognized as being the result of a tough ability to assess the important points and play them well, with all the determination and grit that he possesses.

An interesting anecdote to the story of John Newcombe should also be noted, and that is simply that even the most rational beings are subject to miscalculation. Newcombe's belief in himself became bigger than reality in 1974, his rational appraisal of himself lost some of its validity. For one of the game's biggest hitters to lose twice on grass to an aging Ken Rosewall in significant matches at Wimbledon and Forest Hills must say something. Nineteen hundred seventy-three had been a dramatic year for John Newcombe, but it was over and peaks are hard to maintain. His priorities changed, high competition lost some of its challenge. Subconsciously, he no doubt took the matches for granted, letting up on his training and dedication, losing the edge of his dynamic will to win, projecting the past as a determinant of the future; and that is a fundamental error. At Wimbledon he lost to Rosewall 6-1, 1-6, 6-0, 7-5 in the quarters, and at Forest Hills 6-7, 6-4, 7-6, 6-3 in the semis. Newcombe is untouchable on grass when he is at the top of his game; but he was not in '74, his drive was gone, his investment less. His rational being failed him in that respect. He miscalculated Rosewall but more significantly he miscalculated himself. It takes total commitment to dominate the world—even for John Newcombe.

Stan Smith

Another contemporary personality that I consider one of rational exaggeration is Stan Smith, and the performance that dramatizes this characteristic most fully for me was the 1972 Davis Cup final against Rumania. Smith not only had two formidable foes to contend with but he was facing them on their own ground, two clay court specialists on clay, at home, in Bucharest—literally against 7200 spectators, 11 linesmen, Ilie Nastase and Ion Tiriac. The facts that Stan Smith faced going into this match were simply that Nastase had recently won Forest Hills, that he was recognized by many as the most explosive and talented player in the world, that Rumania had a thirteen match winning streak at home, twelve straight doubles wins, and nineteen straight singles victories for Nastase. The odds seemed considerably against Smith, a hard-hitting fast court player caught away from home on slow clay, playing against as much gamesmanship as the game. Thus the scene was set for the first of Stan Smith's startling performances, an 11-9, 6-2, 6-3 straight set victory over the highly touted Ilie Nastase. Tiriac defeated Tom Gorman in the second match of the series in five sets 4-6, 2-6, 6-4, 6-3, 6-2 to even the match score at one-all. Smith's confidence under pressure was contagious and carried into his doubles match with Erik Vandillen, both playing superlatively to defeat the experienced team of Nastase and Tiriac 6-2, 6-0, 6-3. The outstanding level at which they were playing was apparent to everyone when, during one stretch, they won sixteen out of seventeen games to stake themselves to a 4-1 lead in the third set. But in spite of all of this, the best was yet to come. Smith was soon destined to outdo himself.

His final match of the series was against Tiriac. It was a pivotal match and everyone knew it—the players, the spectators, the world.

Stan Smith

Realizing the significance of the match and willing to do anything to win, Tiriac said, "I am in the match of my life, which is nothing if I lose, no matter how well I play." He was right and he meant to win no matter what, doing whatever was necessary, using everything and everybody at his disposal. He played on his own emotions, the motivation of the crowd, patriotism—there was lots of symbolism at work that day, the atmosphere was electric. It was the kind of situation that inevitably brings out the best or worst in everyone concerned. For four sets Smith and Tiriac played on even terms. But no one could deny that the final set belonged to only one man. It was incredible, and it will stand as a lasting tribute to the iron will and rational character of Stanley Roger Smith. The ability of Smith to appraise himself and the situation accurately is easily recognized as he reflected on his performance during that almost unreal emotional onslaught. He said,

> I've gotta stay calm, ignore the people, ignore anything that Ion does, play the calls regardless of how bad they are, and play my game—hit winners.

Before coming to this conclusion, Smith recognized that he had

> done some very untypical things of me in the fourth set, questioning calls, getting bothered by Tiriac. I lost my composure. During the delays, I let myself wonder if they weren't going to let me win, instead of concentrating on winning.

He concentrated in the fifth set, however, winning it in a fashion that is unlikely to be duplicated. The final score of the match was 4-6, 6-2, 6-4, 2-6, 6-0. Yes, six-love in the fifth! Bud Collins described this final barrage of winners in the following passage:

> In twenty minutes of unbelievable shotmaking—on clay for heaven's sake—beginning with a clear ace, Smith turned Tiriac once again into a 33-year-old hacker, silenced the loyalists, restored the linesmen's eyesight with undeniable winners that put them out of work. Twenty-five of the thirty-three points during the blitz were Smith's, eighteen of them placements plus the inaugural ace. Please don't tell me about the completeness of Tilden after that one. Smith did it all: serve-volley, lung-bursting lobs and drop shots, ripping passing

shots, uncontestable steadiness. On slow clay when he had to score, the smiling carpetbagger from Pasadena made off with the coveted Cup on a 76 percent streak of winners.

Yes, Stan Smith won the Davis Cup for the United States that day. He did so by turning inward, calling on his most rational elements to transcend the distractions of circumstance and to deal positively with the event at hand. It will be a match that will stand as a lasting tribute to the United States, our culture and the strength of character it breeds, but most specifically to Stan Smith—a rational being supreme.

Most players competing on a world class level today can be accurately characterized as some derivative of the professional mentality type, a personality that copes with the competitive act in the most business-like way at his disposal. They approach their activity on the court in this way simply because, in the most real sense, that is exactly what it is. Their activity can only be seen in a true perspective if it is viewed over a length of time, a span longer than that represented by a single match, something more on the order of a ranking year or development of a career to date. These players do not preoccupy themselves with emotionalism on the court and in this way they are very pragmatic. They compute the data of overall success and they act accordingly. They have confidence in their ability but more specifically they have confidence that it will prevail over the long run. These players are so utterly calculated that they are usually successful over the years. They are not flash in the pan champions. Their appearance is one of control, distinctly unemotional, cool as a cucumber. They are Ken Rosewall, Margaret Court, and Chris Evert.

CHAPTER 8

The Professionals

Ken Rosewall

Ken Rosewall has been an interesting phenomenon for the game of tennis because he has literally been ageless, the living spark of an era gone by. His body is one that flows in the most effortless way, probably the greatest stroke master of all time. Psychologically, he is just as steady as his execution on the court. He is the professional's Professional. His mind and body are truly one as he competes, his eyes always directly on the ball, his mind several steps ahead of his opponent, playing out a preconceived master plan, his body flowing in the kind of aesthetic beauty that occasionally allows sport to transcend itself into art form. Rosewall has won almost every accolade that it is possible to win, he has been one of the best players in the world for over twenty years. But in spite of his almost innumerable encounters on the court, the match that depicts, more than any, his "professional" will to win and his calculated approach to the competitive act, was his performance against Rod Laver in 1972, when he won the World Championship of Tennis for the second year in a row.

The past performance charts held Laver as the favorite in this classic encounter, since he had beaten Rosewall soundly in both Toronto and Houston earlier that year. He had beaten the "Little Master" almost every time—except, as we would see, when it really counted; and it counted for plenty that day in Dallas when $50,000 went to the winner then called the world champion of tennis. The final score was 4-6, 6-0, 6-

3, 6-7, 7-6, but the fifth set is where the story is really told. By the time Laver had broken back from 2-4 in the fifth, these two men had been playing under the heat of television lights for over three hours. Dragging feet and slumped shoulders usually typify any Rosewall performance, but as it has turned out so many times before, those physical character-istics were deceptive. Richard Evans wrote in *World Tennis Magazine* . . .

> Rosewall seems about to give in, but once the action starts he is off again. His weary legs get him to the net, not just anyhow but precisely in position to meet one of the best service returns in the game. He volleys not three feet but three inches inside the baseline, as he did in the ninth game of the fifth set.

Rosewall won the ninth game at love with the kind of backhand that has been the measure of his immortality and forced Laver to the limit in the tenth game where he held the first match point of the final. Laver was not to succumb easily, however, saving the match point with an ace down the center and winning the game two points later. There was no question that fatigue was wearing on Rosewall as he dropped the ball tossed to him and wearily debated whether to bend over and get it. Again, however, it was a different story when the ball was in play, deep angled serves and firm volleys. The tired little man was to hold serve at love for the second time in a row. Laver countered with the flamboy-ance of a different style to tie the score in games again and the ultimate scene was then set—sudden death in the fifth. Laver began the tie breaker decisively, holding a 3-1 and 5-3 lead, only two points from vic-tory, yet two Rosewallian backhands evened the score at 5-all. Laver continued his assault of one of the finest strokes ever developed, Rose-wall's backhand, and he paid a heavy price for it. It was a simple error in judgment but at that time it was a costly one. Three hours and thirty-four minutes is a long time and the match produced an incredible amount of mental and physical strain. The last point where Laver blooped an easy return into the net seemed anticlimactic but it was also a testament of the intensity at which these two men had been playing, and that even the best are fallible and have limits. Rosewall exemplified professionalism of the first order that day, investing so much of him-self, gutting it out to the very end, the epitome of mental and physical discipline. Kenny did a job that day.

Ken Rosewall   (Photo: Russ Adams Prod.)

Margaret Court

Margaret Court could possibly be the greatest female player of all time. Certainly, her record over the years speaks for itself. Since 1960 she has amassed an incredible thirty-three singles titles in the world's most prestigious tournaments—three Wimbledon, five United States, five French, three Italian, three South African, eleven Australian and three German. Remarkable consistency and durability over the years, exactly what one would expect from the "professional" mentality. Margaret is well aware of her talent and she counts on it prevailing in the long run. It is a point of fact that she possesses one of the finest bodies ever at the disposal of a tennis player—the embodiment of pure athleticism, the natural athlete; lean and strong and quick, reminding one of the uncanny movements of a gazelle or cheetah on an African plain. But along with this wonderful gift, Margaret's personality also represents a bit of a paradox. She is very much a woman and values much of the traditional feminine role—husband and children taking priority even over her tennis. It was this sensitive side of her that was taken advantage of in her match with Bobby Riggs, and it was her acceptance of her defeat and her reorientation to the future that really showed the professionalism of her nature. She was never an adamant women's libber, it was not her cause. She was happy being a woman, playing women on women's terms, and she was the best at that. So all the implications of the "Battle of the Sexes" was a bit foreign. Her response to her loss that day was inspirational, her bad loss, yet . . . even her humiliation, on Mother's Day, bearing a cross that wasn't even her own. She had had a spectacular year before that match and she continued her winning ways after it. Her self image was not threatened by one out of proportion match. She believed in what she was doing and that she was the best woman player in the world. She was proud of it and proving it was no problem. She did it every time she went to the court.

In 1972 Margaret Court ended the year by soundly defeating everyone in sight. There was no question in anyone's mind who was the best player in the world. Her overall record against the nine other women ranked in the top ten in the world was thirty-two wins and three losses. She was 2-1 against Evert, 3-1 against Billie Jean King, 5-0 against Evonne Goolagong, 6-0 against Kerry Melville, 5-0 against Virginia Wade, 9-0 against Rosemary Casals, 1-0 against Olga Morozova, and 1-1 against Nancy Gunter—truly a remarkable year, clearly dominating the world. She won the Australian Open, the French Open, the United

Margaret Court

States Open, and thirteen Virginia Slims events. She won on all surfaces against all comers. This kind of consistency is a true mark of a professional because it is not a fluctuating mentality. It is not subject to moods or great days and terrible ones. Professionals are constant. Their personalities are stable and their capacity to play long matches or tough tournaments to the end is their hallmark. An example of this stick-to-itiveness factor was illustrated in the 1973 French Championships during her final against Chris Evert. She spotted Evert twelve years and five months, and was a set and 3-5 down in the second before coming back to win in a typical two hour and fifteen minute thriller. The "professional" is a dedicated athlete with a strong will to win. Only Suzanne Lenglen had won the French title five times before Margaret decided to write one more star beside her name in the record books.

The 1973 United States Open was also a typical hard-nosed Margaret Court showing. In the quarters she defeated Virginia Wade 7-6, 7-6, causing her opponent to lament, "Why doesn't anyone ever crumble against me?" In the semis she played Christ Evert and this match offers particular insight into her problem-solving nature. She won 7-5, 2-6, 6-2, but only through the most conscientious mental discipline to bide her time, approach the net carefully, being patient enough to face up to those endless Evert rallies from the baseline in order to crack the armour enough to take the net. That was the plan she stuck to in the first set, leading 5-2 before reverting to her more natural hard hitting style. Evert evened the score at 5-all, before Court tones herself down enough to close the set out at 7-5. She attacked with impatience again in the second set and lost it 6-2. In the third set she realized her failing and solved the problem for good, closing out the match six games to two, in a typically deliberate effort.

Linda Timms wrote in *World Tennis Magazine* that Court's final against Evonne Goolagong was ". . . surely one of the best matches Margaret has ever played." She herself compared it to her classic defeat of Billie Jean King in the 1970 Wimbledon final. She began the match quickly, staking herself to a 3-0 and 4-1 lead. It takes a challenge to get the most out of Margaret Court, the fact that she got off to such a quick start working against her to the point that it took a tie breaker to close the set out. She was coasting on that momentum to lead 4-2 in the second, when the grace and cool of Goolagong found its range to even the match at a set apiece, 7-5. She could have dwelled on the fact that she had blown a chance to close out the match earlier, decisively. She didn't, however. Instead, she bore down and went back to work. Margaret

Court is a person who invests a lot of herself in herself. This all important but intangible factor of pride is what makes her the truest of professionals . . . and possibly the greatest woman player of all time.

Chris Evert

Christ Evert is like a machine. She is also the embodiment of paradox, her sweet "little girl" rise to fame and her poker-faced, iron-willed concentration presenting an interesting study in contradiction. Watching Chris Evert has somehow been like watching Shirley Temple outdraw Jesse James in a Texas shootout. Sweet little girls aren't supposed to be out conquering the world, yet at the young age of sixteen Chrissie, everybody's All American dream, began toppling the world's best. She grew up on Florida clay, learning that steadiness wins when the surface is slow, and that it takes real mental discipline to perfect a game of that style. Both elements came naturally for her, the slow clay and the methodical nature that makes her such a study in professionalism. Definitely mature beyond her years, she induces one to think that only the most unusual circumstances would be at work for her to miss or to lose. She looms like a heavy fog across the baseline, smothering the ball like it was her own, collecting it on her racket and firing it back down the line or crosscourt with a confidence and demeanor all her own. Her pinpoint placements write their own story, hundreds of marks in clay inches from the lines, her two handed backhand now as American as double-dip ice cream cones. She rose fast but she is not a flash in the pan, in-and-out champion. Her strokes are rock solid, like a most efficient machine. Her temperament is unchanging, distinctly unemotional, very businesslike, very "professional." Chris Evert never beats herself. The pressure she creates is relentless because she is so unlikely to make mistakes, that bad days are simply something you don't count on or realistically hope for. If you beat Chris Evert, you have to do just that—beat her, hit through her, attack the net, hit winners. She is the steadiest player in the world, she is one of the best slow court artists of all time, and she is all of that because of her steadfast temperament. No one concentrates like this young lady, for it takes real mental discipline to use her arsenal of shots the way she does. Her professionalism tells her that her talent will prevail, that machines rarely break down, that they are very efficient tools. And what chance do mortal women have against that icy cool of a computer.

A match that depicts Evert's analytical approach and her tough will to win occurred at Wimbledon in 1974 in the second round against Lesley Hunt. It had to have been the most exciting match of the tournament, Evert prevailing in three hard sets and two hours and forty-six minutes, 8-6, 5-7, 11-9. Rex Bellamy wrote in *The Times* (London) the following description:

> The tennis was always richly entertaining and often magical in its breathtaking blend of skill and drama—with a sharp contrast of personalities and playing styles to add flavor to the feast. In the third set, thrills flocked upon us, numbing the nerves, as Evert twice served for the match and three times served to save it. Both players gave so much in terms of skill and will, physical and nervous energy, that it eventually became emotionally exhausting merely to watch them.

The contrast of character was not hard to notice—Evert's femininity, her ribboned hair and dress trimmed to match; Hunt, the uninhibited, hard hitting tomboy, the embodiment of exuberance and health and love of just plain knocking the cover off the ball. Their personalities were in contrast and so were their playing styles. Evert depended on her characteristic chalk-dusting drives, venturing, as the closeness of the match beckoned, into a more uncharacteristic variety of shot making, crisp volleys and even drop shot service returns. Hunt's natural flair for the spectacular no doubt forced Evert into this deviation of style. Bellamy recounts that intangible but lasting quality of the match . . .

> It was no time for statistics, for stripping a marvelous match to the dry bones of detailed analysis. It was time to sit back and let the heart sing.

To most the resumption of the match at nine all the next day was anticlimactic. But it was between the days, during the interval, that the ultimate difference was made. Evert's sensitivity for analysis led her to review Hunt's pattern of play on television. Patterns repeat themselves. She was prepared, she was able to counter Hunt's strategy with indicatives rather than responses—in short, her pragmatism paid off. When the match resumed, she immediately won two straight games and the match 8-6, 5-7, 11-9. And that is the "professional" way.

In 1974, Chris Evert was ranked as the Number One player in the world. While only twenty years old, she was in the "summer of her

Chris Evert

talent," carrying herself similar to the way she did at Forest Hills in 1971, when at sixteen years she first captured the imagination of the world. Since then, she and her tennis game have both matured. Formerly rather one-dimensionally oriented at the baseline, she now possesses the striking marks of all court competence. They say she misses fewer shots from the backcourt than a metronome skips a beat, but that is nothing new. To complement this basic style, she has improved her volley and her serve, the latter of which is characterized by some as one of the most strategically placed in the game. Add to this a touch of velvet on her drop shot and lob and one has a hand-picked game of unusual versatility and completeness. It is precisely the kind of game that is sound and consistent enough to lead a player to a 56 match winning streak in international competition. For Chris Evert to compile such a remarkable record in 1974 speaks directly of her perfectionist nature— certainly a dominant part of the "professional mentality." In 1974, she won everything in sight on clay: Fort Lauderdale, Sarasota, St. Petersburg, The Family Circle Cup, the U.S. Clay, the Canadian Open, the Italian, and the French. Her year continued flawlessly as she made the transition to grass without a stumble, wining Eastbourne and then Wimbledon. At Wimbledon, she lost 22 games in her spectacular effort against Lesley Hunt, only lost 23 in her remaining five. Chris Evert has introduced to us one of the most dominating competitive spirits in the game. She is match tough and she is very much the "professional." Count on her being around a long time.

CHAPTER 9

The Shotmakers

On the sign it is written
Don't pick the blossom
But it is useless against the wind
Which cannot read.

Thus we have the shotmakers, the talented athletes, those whose gift is superior, whose command over their bodies is most profound, natural and complete, effortless and spontaneous. These personalities do not appear conscious and deliberate. They have lived with their talent all their lives, they know no other way, and because of that fact they trust it. This is a very important idea, one that is entirely different from those players who out of necessity must think, must solve the physical problems, cannot rely so fully on the unspoken, unknown, but undeniable intangible of natural talent. It just works, that's all. If they want it, they try it, the spectacular shots fall in. There is no other way. These are the eccentric champions, those in the zone, out of their heads players. As a rule they are not as consistent as those more deliberate players. They are hot and cold, capable of beating anyone anywhere but just as capable of losing. They often respond to their moods, and emotions always fluctuate. These are the spontaneous personalities, the fluid, graceful, beautiful athletes. These are the ones through which sport sometimes transcends itself into art form. These are the players who bring the aesthetic quality to the game, the wonderful fluidity of grace. They are the unforgettable and undeniable. They are geniuses and they embody all that is beautiful and free. They are Evonne Goolagong and Ilie Nastase.

Evonne Goolagong

There may have never been a female player to possess the natural talent of Evonne Goolagong. Her gift has been more than profound. Like a reed in the wind, her body moves in unmatched fluidity and grace. She is able to acknowledge and adapt to her circumstance on the court in only the most spontaneous way. When she engages in the act of playing the game, she transforms a physical problem-solving exercise into art. Here is a genius truly unmatched, the most natural, an act of nature more than any. Her strength and speed and assurance are second to none, like a falcon soaring in utter command of the wind. The ancient philosophers of Greece addressed themselves specifically to the human spirit we see in Evonne Goolagong. They immortalized the humanness of the human spirit, worshipping man with an optimistic fervor that died long ago. Their statues were perfect specimens of bodily proportion, they invented the Olympic Games as the ultimate test of humanity, of heaven on earth, for oak clusters, laurel wreaths and godliness. They would have reveled in the beauty of Evonne Goolagong as she plays.

When Evonne "has it together" there is no other. There is no conscious preoccupation with thought. It simply happens. Consistency in concentration has been difficult for her, however, for that is the nature of spontaneity, because it is by definition unplanned, uncontrolled and beyond willful direction and manipulation. She calls her lapses "walk abouts," but what you call them is irrelevant. Her mental preoccupation is as much a part of her as her flair for spectacular shot-making. It is inherent in the mentality, part of her genius, as natural as any imperfection is in any human endeavor. She won Wimbledon when she was only nineteen years old in a prodigal achievement that served notice to all that the game had certainly been blessed, that there were to be beautiful years ahead of shots unseen and unknown and unplanned until their executioner felt and expressed them. Every time this young champion goes on the court the heart sings in this anticipation, of the potential of the future, like a wonderful gift that illuminates the boundless and universal potential within us all.

Her classic duels with Chris Evert have often brought out her best, and her semi-final victory at Forest Hills in 1974 was certainly no excep-

Evonne Goolagong

tion. Francis Harden has commented that Evert and Goolagong represent a contrast between "the cerebral and the sensual, concentration and inspiration, method and mood, classic music and jazz." These are good analogies and they are contrasts that have often combined to give us peak performance from both players. Evert had won 56 straight singles matches going into this particular encounter and had not lost a set since she defeated Lesley Hunt in the second round at Wimbledon. Rain interrupted the match for two days with Goolagong leading 6-0, 4-3. Commenting on Goolagong's spectacular first set, Rex Bellamy says, "Women's tennis offers no spectacle more enchanting than Goolagong playing well. In the first set her game has flexibly imaginative facility, a purring smoothness, an inborn assurance of expressing herself in her own medium." When the match resumed Goolagong had two match points at 5-3 against service and was to later serve for the match in a long game that contained two controversial calls. She broke serve again, but Evert matched the effort to tie the score at six-all. In the tie breaker she led three points to one but lost four in a row to drop the set. A quick burst at the beginning of the third set, where she won the first three games with the loss of only four points, however, staked her to a lead she would never relinquish. Concentration and unmatched talent merged that day as Evonne played, and it staked her to an impressive win when the cards were on the table and the chips down. She won 6-0, 6-7, 6-3 in just one more demonstration of the reality of the intangible—of fluid spontaneity and grace, of art, and beauty as it can exist on a tennis court.

Ilie Nastase

Ilie Nastase is the original "bad boy" of tennis, a man-child, the most mature of talents, the most impish of attitudes. No one can seriously question his gift of talent, for his speed of foot and his quickness of hand are at times unmatched. He is a shotmaker by nature, an eccentric, an explosive artist who loves to defy the reality of circumstance, to defy pressure and all the percentages of conservatism. The tactics and strategy that he employs are only his own. He is not one who defines his own strengths in terms of opponent weaknesses to form a master plan of attack. He is never that deliberate. His tennis simply happens, and when it does it happens so well that strategies are unnecessary and defenses useless. His shotmaking when in "the zone" is so utterly unpredictable and spectacular that attempts for his opposition to reason and solve the

Ilie Nastase

problems of defense are futile. His shots are too good, and they follow no logical pattern. Patterns are definable, can be anticipated and can be countered. They are rational. Nastase is not a rational being by any means. He doesn't play rationally and he doesn't act rationally either. Indeed, his behavior often borders on the irrational as he indulges himself in a reception to emotion that is all but immoral in degree. Tradition has held tennis to be a game of etiquette and manner, a gentleman's game, of crisp whites on fine green lawns. Contemporary tennis, however, certainly denotes a marked difference from that standard, and whether the changes themselves spawned the development of personalities like Nastase, or whether people like him brought about the change is debatable. Nevertheless, the facts remain the same, the game is now characterized by color in the most literal and abstract ways, red shirts and fiery emotion neither being uncommon.

Nastase's outbursts of emotion have affected different people in different ways. The press loves him because he adds controversy to a traditionally mild-mannered sport. Tennis loyalists, however, find Ilie Nastase a tough pill to swallow sometimes. Neil Amdur, for example, writes—"I've had it with Ilie Nastase. I'm tired of seeing him pampered, fined, reprimanded, censured, scolded. The time has come to put Ilie Nastase in his place, to tell him what he should already know about the game—that it's bigger than any hot shot dude. The time has come to tell Nasty, as he has been so affectionally christened in some circles, one more outburst, one more serious series of insults will cost him more than dollars and cents, which he already has plenty of: It will cost him one full year of playing ANY tennis in the United States. That's right, banishment from the game for one year." His list of offenses goes on, Amdur compiling what he calls a "bill of particulars" in the case against Ilie Nastase. It reads as follows:

A BILL OF PARTICULARS
The Case Against Ilie Nastase

A partial listing of his offenses against the game, the spectators and his fellow competitors:

1969
NICE
In a mixed doubles match, Nastase twice smashes volleys from close range into Gail Chanfreau of France. She retaliates by hurling her racket at him.

WIMBLEDON
During a Davis Cup match against Mark Cox of Britain, Nastase becomes enraged at a linesman's call. He stomps around the court, kicks a chair, rattles his rackets, and later gives what he calls "the Balkan peace sign" to the crowd.

1971
NICE
Nastase puts Jan Kodes of Czechoslovakia completely off his game in a final round match by complaining about decisions, badgering officials and threatening to walk off the court. He also wins the match.

PARIS
In the finals of a Grand Prix event, Nastase's behavior provokes the United States' Cliff Richey to such an extent that they almost wind up swinging more than rackets.

1972
LONDON
At Albert Hall, Clark Graebner of the United States becomes so infuriated at Nastase's antics during a match that he climbs over the net, jabs Nastase in the chest and warns him about future shenanigans. Nastase walks off saying, "I am too frightened to continue."

ROME
Nastase's petulant behavior in a men's doubles final causes a near riot. Police are summoned to prevent irate spectators from storming the court.

BUCHAREST

In the Davis Cup final round against the United States, Nastase glares, complains and engages in frenzied monologues as Stan Smith routs him before his home crowd. Afterward, he blames his defeat on a blister. And then he chokes miserably in a doubles match.

1973

SALISBURY, MD.

After a few early line calls go against him at the United States Indoor Championships in a quarter final match against Brian Gottfried, Nastase gives up. He aims serves at linesmen, hits balls far beyond the baseline and stands motionless as shots bounce near him. Says veteran official Mke Blanchard: "I've never seen anything worse." Later, the U.S.L.T.A. fines Nastase $1000.

CINCINNATI

At the Western Open, playing against Manuel Orantes, Nastase hits balls at linesmen, curses the referee and refuses to resume play when ordered. The U.S.L.T.A. later fines him $4500.

FOREST HILLS

Nastase quits the doubles of the United States Open Championships after having been upset in singles.

The unique combination of talent and temperament that has come together to make Ilie Nastase what he is may at times seem unethical and hard to live with, but, in spite of it all, it and he does win. He is simply one more individual mentality that comes out on top. A case in point that illustrates the controversial nature of his winning method was certainly his final match against Arthur Ashe at Forest Hills in 1972. The stage was set in an extraordinary way from the very beginning, with two men as different as night and day, backgrounds and personalities in total contrast, facing each other across the net for $25,000 and a national championship. Ashe, known by many as "Mr. Cool," is characteristically calm and analytical in his approach. Nastase, on the other hand, is high strung, easily excited, an immature prankster and "incurable hot dog." Says Barry Lorge—"When things go wrong on the court, he misbehaves and stomps his foot; when he wins he is a kid playing in a sandbox, and sometimes that means he throws sand at his playmates."

Both players came into the match impressively, Ashe cracking his service returns decisively enough to carry him to straight set victories over both Stan Smith and Cliff Richey. Nastase had not lost a match since the week after Wimbledon leading Rumania past both the Soviet Union and Australia in the Davis Cup. In August he won the Canadian Open and the Eastern Grass Courts in Orange, New Jersey. The past performance charts would lay the edge to Ashe on grass but Nastase's quickness and touch made him a threat to anyone anywhere. At his best Ilie is incredible, chasing down shots most players would concede and slashing them back for impossible winners. But because he has a history of often being just as scatterbrained as he is talented, he sometimes comes out on the short end of the score. No one ever knows where his fragile concentration may end up. His best is unsurpassed, his worst is terrible. This particular match was unusual because all of Ilie Nastase's sides showed themselves; the "Peck's Bad Boy" behavior, as well as the spectacular shotmaking—all the eccentricities of genius at once.

His concentration seemed lost early when he became distracted over a footfault call, his composure apparently lost for good later in the third set tie breaker when he argued and lost a disputed service call. In retaliation he flipped a towel at linesman Jack Stahr and then hit a ball at him after holding serve to begin the fourth set. When he then proceeded to fall behind 1-3, he decided to express his general disapproval with the state of the world by flashing what he calls "the Balkan peace sign," a sign that is known to most others as an obscene gesture. His atmosphere of villany thus created with 14,000 fans solidly against him, Nastase was then able to work with his devil-may-care attitude that said to everyone, including his opponent, that he felt he had everything to gain and nothing to lose, and that was not fair from the truth side. After all, Ashe was only two service games from victory. Serving at 5-3 Ashe came back from 0-4 but still dropped the game to lose his service. Nastase's loose play was threatening Ashe who, whether it be fact or fiction, thought he saw it all slipping away. Fiction began to show signs of fact when he lost the fourth set with a grossly miss-hit smash and both players knew it. Ashe became despondent and then frantic in his effort to regrasp what he had thought he had already won. Nastase had inadvertently put Ashe into the only position that could threaten him that day, for Ashe's desperation soon spawned errors and turned the tide against him. The flame of exaggerated confidence was soon lit for Nastase and his genius began to peak. When he got to the net, Arthur's passing shots had to dust chalk to get by. Shots came off Ashe's racket that deserved no return—but Ilie was there, blocking and returning with incredible precision. A decisive turning point in the match had to be when Ashe was serving at 2-3, 30-all and slipped in the process of hitting an almost sure putaway with his backhand at the net. The reality of that error no doubt combined with his already acute preoccupation with Nastase's new momentum, causing him to hit another long volley and fall behind 2-4. On match point at 5-3, Ashe ripped a backhand return into the top of the net that somehow managed to climb over, trickling for an apparent lucky winner onto Nastase's side. Everyone had conceded the point and had begun to breathe again—everyone, that is, except one person. Nastase appeared from nowhere, like lightning, like the mythological Mercury, touching the ball back into Ashe's court for the most spectacular of wins. It was an incredible ending to an incredible match. All the sides of Ilie were on display that day—but the one that will be remembered the longest will, of course, be the fact of the obvious. Ilie Nastase won Forest Hills in 1972.

CHAPTER 10

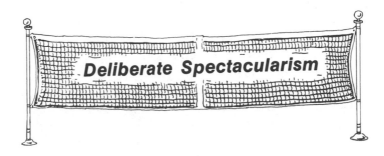

Deliberate Spectacularism

Rod Laver has a history of being deliberately spectacular, a characteristic of play that is of a decidedly different nature than either the entirely rational side of being deliberate, or the completely spontaneous nature of spectacularism. John Newcombe, for example, is deliberate, but he makes very realistic on-the-court decisions that win points with a minimum amount of risk. He is a rational percentage player who has the capacity for great shotmaking but whose most fundamental priorities always lie in winning, accomplishing the winning act in the most economical way possible. Ilie Nastase, on the other hand, floats in and out of the spontaneously spectacular zone with no deliberate thought at all. Laver represents a cross-section of sorts, a rather unique combination of the two extremes, not only having that remarkable capacity for unbelievable shotmaking but having the apparent ability to call on his repertoire of greatness almost at will. It's like Laver might say to himself on the ninth point of a tie breaker—"Well, Rocket, I think it's time for the 'Rod Laver 100 mph backhand topspin cross court angle'." Without a doubt, the mentality that exercises deliberate greatness is an enviable one. Laver has dominated the game in his era, he was the only Grand Slam winner in the history of the game. It is the deliberate greatness that Rod Laver represents that is so interesting because, as even the most objective analysis reveals, it was so utterly consistent. An innate confidence of the first order merging with a superior physical talent to bring greatness in large doses, over a period of time, dominance not in single matches but over every player in the world for extended periods, for seasons and years. The act of winning a Grand Slam, for example, is infinitely difficult. A player must win all four of the world's biggest tournaments in the same year (Australian, French, Wimbledon, United States) to accomplish such a feat, an act that requires defeating all comers on both slow and fast surfaces. Don Budge was the first player to do it in 1938 and Laver followed in 1962 and in 1969. Deliberate spectacularism represents greatness in the most profound way for it is representative more than any of *consistent dominance*, dominance with a flair, completeness, a perfection of sorts, class that spawned some of the most profound results of all. His story is written in all the record books and it is a story of excellence; of discipline and dedication and work that found its reward and left an indelible mark.

It can be legitimately argued that Rod Laver is the greatest player of all time. His record certainly stands out above the rest, two of the three Grand Slams ever won being his. He has been a dominant force in the game for over fifteen years, his flaming red hair, soft spoken demeanor and huge left arm a trademark familiar to even the most casual observer. He has always been a force to be contended with, always near the top, a persistent obstacle to anyone with aspirations of being Number One. In 1962, 1969, and 1971, he demonstrated that he could be literally unbeatable, spectacular shots and strings of matches becoming quite the norm as he seemed to own every player on the international circuit. His lopsided dominance of the game caused Fred Podesta to state in 1971 that "On one of his very best days, Bill Tilden *might* have had a chance against Laver." Laver did unheard of things to the ball in his peak years, using his circumstance on the court to achieve a personal perfection of sorts, forcing his opponents into submission with unmatched flair, Laverian genius. Julius Heldman described his decisive approach as follows: "Rod swings at everything hard and fast. His timing, eye, and wrist action are nothing short of miraculous. On either side, forehand or backhand, he takes a full roundhouse loop crack at the ball, which comes back so hard that it can knock the racket out of your hand. I saw Rafe Ossuna in the semi finals at Forest Hills in 1962. It was murder. In the last game Rafe bravely served and ran for the net. Rod cracked a backhand back full speed, free swing—so hard that Rafe's racket wavered in his hand. Not so amazing perhaps but the same scene was repeated four points in a row. Rod literally knocked Osuna down with four successive returns and Osuna was one of the quickest and best racket handlers that ever played the game."

Rod Laver   (Photo: Assoc. of Tennis Professionals)

The momentum for Laver's first Grand Slam began in 1961 when he defeated Chuck McKinley in the finals of Wimbledon 6-3, 6-1, 6-4, a match that only lasted fifty-five minutes. McKinley managed to win only ten points in the second set which took a mere thirteen minutes to complete. At four-all in the final set, McKinley found himself on the receiving end of a typical Lavarian holocaust. Says Fred Tupper, "He slapped a backhand down the line, banked a forehand down the other and then hammered a backhand squarely into the corner—three outright winners. McKinley hadn't touched one." The context of this outburst and other similar ones leads one to believe he simply decided that it was time—time to again call on the reality of his confidence. John Newcombe said in 1971, "When I make a truly great shot I look up and thank God. Rod takes his for granted." And Newcombe's appraisal would seem to be accurate. But while he may appear to take his shot-making for granted, it should also be noted that he does not wear his confidence shabbily. He is not an obnoxious winner. He is the original humble champion. Exhibition of exaggerated confidence almost always finds its way to the surface with achievement at this level, but Rod Laver proves, here, that he is again quite the exception to the rule. Fred Perry, the great British player and Wimbledon champion in 1934, 1935 and 1936, feels that the reality of Laver's confidence first showed itself in the finals of the French championships in 1961. Against his Australian Davis Cup teammate Roy Emerson, Laver was trailing two sets to love and 4-5 on Emerson's serve before rallying to win the set and the match to keep alive his hopes for the Grand Slam. "You could see his confidence bloom after that," said Perry, "it was just like the petals of a flower opening up."

In 1968 Laver defeated Tony Roche 6-3, 6-4, 6-2 to win the first "open" Wimbledon, a win noteworthy not only because it was the first open championship held there but because of the decisive way in which he captured it. His reputation was not lacking before that, certainly, for as an amateur he had already won the six biggest tournaments in the world in the same year, (Australian, Italian, French, Wimbledon, German, United States). Be that as it may, consensus of opinion never holds this performance against Roche as one of his best. Says Lance Tingay, "How galling it must have been for him (Roche) to play his heart out, to reach standards of stroking that were first class only to be permitted merely an ignominious hour on the court." In 1961 Laver won his first Wimbledon by defeating Chuck McKinley for the loss of eight games, and in 1962 he duplicated his victory by losing only five to

Martin Mulligan. Tony Roche managed to steal nine in 1968, a feat that caused Tingay to conclude his statement of the match by saying simply "The highest tribute I can pay Roche is that he did well enough to make Laver bring out his finest game." And maybe that's all one could expect. Laver was peaking again, the flamboyance of his style taking the game by storm. His momentum continued to grow, leading him decisively into his second Grand Slam the next year. He concluded the last leg of his feat against Roche again, this time in the finals of Forest Hills, 5-7, 6-1, 6-2, 6-2. It was getting to the point where it was difficult to even conceive anyone other than Laver winning, especially when it counted, when the stakes were the largest. He peaked deliberately for big tournaments, big matches, big points. He made calculated decisions of greatness, a truly unique study in confidence and control. His dominance appeared so profound at this point that Roy Blount said, "It looks as though the sport will have to be opened considerably wider, to include angels, highly trained kangaroos or something yet unenvisaged, before anyone else will be Laver's league." Rod Laver's control of the spectacular was indeed beginning to show signs of the heavenly—and there were no other angels around to challenge him.

By 1971 you would have thought that the incentive for perfection might have diminished, that it had all been won before, that some of the luster would be gone. That was not to be the case. In 1971 a unique event called the Tennis Champions' Classic assembled a field of the best players in the world to play a series of winner-take-all matches for $160,000. In essence, it was head on head competition for big money— "all the cash." The probability of anyone winning thirteen matches in a row against Ken Rosewall, John Newcombe, Tony Roche, Roy Emerson, Arthur Ashe, Tom Okker, Roger Taylor, and Dennis Ralston was just incredibly small. The field was too good, the incentive too great for any mortal human being, that is. The world of tennis watched the heavenly become real again when Rod Laver won it all, however, every single match, complete dominance, another Laverian assertion of perfection.

Jan. 2, 1971	def.	Ken Rosewall 6-3, 6-2, 7-5
Jan. 9, 1971	def.	John Newcombe 6-4, 6-2, 4-6, 5-7, 6-4
Jan. 13, 1971	def.	Tony Roche 7-5, 4-6, 3-6, 7-5, 6-1
Jan. 16, 1971	def.	Roy Emerson 6-2, 6-3, 7-5
Jan. 21, 1971	def.	Tom Okker 5-7, 5-7, 6-2, 6-2, 6-2
Jan. 28, 1971	def.	Arthur Ashe 3-6, 6-3, 6-3, 6-4

Feb. 3, 1971	def.	Roger Taylor 6-3, 7-5, 6-2
Feb. 6, 1971	def.	Tom Okker 6-1, 6-4, 6-3
Feb. 17, 1971	def.	Dennis Ralston 3-6, 6-1, 6-4, 6-3
Feb. 19, 1971	def.	Roy Emerson 6-3, 5-7, 6-3, 3-6, 6-3
March 18, 1971	def.	Dennis Ralston 6-3, 6-4, 7-5
March 19, 1971	def.	Tom Okker 7-5, 6-2, 6-1

"At the very outset," said Laver, "I totally agreed with everyone that it was virtually impossible for any one player to go through this Classic undefeated. I have done just that—and I do not believe it either."

Any story of Red Laver will depict him as a master. Physically, his talent is obvious; chalk-dusting drives where compromise is unknown, services of precision, looping topspin implemented with delicate touch. His timing, speed, and wrist action are unsurpassed, all his own. The only thing more profound than Rod Laver's physical talent on the court is his mental game, the side of him that frees his talent to do what it does, that permits spectacularism, and permits it when it is needed most. Rod Laver is the best example of *deliberate* greatness to be found, an almost romantic story of soft-spoken flamboyance—idealism that was real.

CHAPTER 11

Don Budge's on court performance and psychological motivation is much like the deliberate greatness of Rod Laver. He was a player who picked his spots well, who knew the big matches and tournaments and worked to play them well in the most calculated fashion. He was the first winner of the Grand Slam of tennis, a showing of world dominance more than any. But more prominent, even, than his deliberate efforts, one must recognize the most honorable way in which he carried himself. He was part of an era gone by where idealism was noble and romanticism real. And he was the best. It was a time dominated by great leaders—Roosevelt, Churchill, Stalin, Hitler—unusual men with romantic ideals to uphold. In tennis, these were the glorious years of etiquette, long flannels, white shoes, and cable knit sweaters—the years of nationalism, of patriotic obligation, of the Davis Cup. Don Budge played tennis in a time when American idealism was popular and he was the All-American sportsman, humble but firm, clean cut and proper.

The continuity and firmness of the Budge personality was directly reflected in his approach to the ball. His style was just as straightforward as his appearance. The essence of his game originated at the baseline, a hard hitter whose forte was sustained power off the ground. His forehand was traditional, bordering on the mechanical, as he hit from his closed stance, driving the ball crosscourt or down the line with equal authority. His backhand is thought by many to be the most outstanding single stroke ever developed. Julius D. Heldman said, "Budge's back-hand is the most famous ground stroke in tennis. Technically, it was very much like his forehand, but it had that extra flair, that great freedom of motion, which made it the envy of every player who ever lived." Heldman stated further that "He was the King of the Tennis World from 1937 until World War II and to those of us who were on the circuit with him he was not only untouchable but the greatest player of all time."

Superlatives like the above do not go totally unfounded, it should be noted, especially when one considers the level of play he demonstrated as he defeated Baron Gottfried von Cramm when the United States challenged Germany for the Davis Cup in 1937. Budge himself said, "I find no difficulty whatever in naming the greatest tennis match I ever played in. I know that I never played better tennis, nor did I ever play anyone as good as Cramm. Walter Pate, the United States team captain, said later, 'No other player—living or dead—could have beaten either man that day.' " It was a pivotal match since the overall team score was tied at two-all. The atmosphere was charged with emotion from the start, not only because the winner would earn the chance to face England for the Cup, but because of the nationalistic fervor that was so prevalent at the time. One should not forget the impact of Jesse Owens the year before when, as a non-Aryan he so damaged the pride of Adolf Hitler at the Olympic Games in Berlin. To win the Davis Cup, at this time, would certainly be a shot in the arm for Aryan philosophy and propaganda. It was the kind of situation that could bring out the best or worst in everyone involved. In this case it brought out the best in both men, for both played with an intensity of purpose that spawned a level of play that may never be duplicated, possibly the greatest match of all time.

Budge led 5-4 in the first set, hit four good first serves in the tenth game, but lost it at love when Cramm broke back with four outright winners on the return. The caliber of play was rising steadily on the part of both men with Budge eventually dropping the set 8-6. He said, "It was a little discouraging. I was sure that I was playing tennis as well as I ever had before, but here I was one set down and struggling to stay even in the second. The fewer mistakes I made, he made fewer still." At 5-6 in the second set Budge staked himself to a 40-love advantage but let it slip by. They battled through two more advantages until, for the first time, Cramm had a set point. In retrospect it would seem that he knew it too for he was not timid in the way he played it, following Budge's serve

Don Budge   (Photo: USTA)

to the net and taking his return in "go for broke" fashion, a volley that raised chalk on the back line. Budge said, "At this point, I remember being more angry than analytical and that may have been a good thing for I promptly went out and broke his serve in the first game of the third set."

He got his break and he never relinquished it, as he ran out the set 6-4, continuing his momentum and later winning the fourth, 6-2. Entering a fifth set with Cramm was something to think about because his record in five set matches to date had been all but unbelievable. Only a few days before he had brought himself from the brink of defeat in a key match against Czechoslovakia in the finals of the European Zone, 3-6, 4-6, 6-4, 6-3, 6-2. In the French Championships the year before he went five sets in almost all of his matches before winning the tournament 6-0 in the fifth over the famous British champion, Fred Perry. It was a fact that must have entered Budge's mind in that final set for despite his efforts to maintain the momentum he had gained, he fell behind 1-4. It was here, as the players changed courts, that Budge made a statement that has since become a part of tennis folklore. He said, "Don't count us out yet, Cap. Look, I'm not tired and I feel great." From this point, Budge went on to win the next eight points in a row, no small feat against an opponent who was still playing magnificently with victory well in sight. Al Laney said, "We must count this as one of the finest moments the game has known and I have never seen a champion in any sport do a better thing at so critical a moment." Budge knew how close he was to defeat and with that in mind, changed his response to Cramm's service. His decision was to creep several steps inside the baseline on the second serve, attack it and follow it to the net. His new strategy brought him to 3-4, with each of the four points won being on well-placed volleys on the second shot. At four games all, the tension grew but both players rose to the occasion. They matched serves until six-all, when Budge finally broke, for the first time really leading in the match. Cramm had not only led two sets to none but had been ahead 5-4 and 6-5 in the fifth. The last point of the match has been remembered as the finest, certainly a fitting conclusion to such an immortal encounter. Budge described that final point in the following passage:

"So once more I served. It was the 175th time that day I had made a first serve. what there had been of my cannonball had gone, but I managed to get enough on this one to clear the net and send it sufficiently deep so that Gottfried could not begin to move up and gain the net from me. But he made a beautiful long return that kept me far back in the court too. All I could do was trade long ground strokes with him. I hit a good backhand.

"Cramm moved over to his right corner, so that we were both on the same side of the court—facing each other down my left side. He caught my shot with a forehand and hit it crosscourt. It was a beautiful shot, firmly hit, and it gave him an opening to move toward the net. He came up, crossing the court catty-cornered, following, essentially, the direction of his shot.

"The ball was landing just inside my right sideline, a bit deep of midcourt. I had hit my last shot far back on the other side of the court and I had begun to move toward the center as soon as I hit it. Now, however, when I saw Cramm place the ball so far over, I had to break into a dead run if I wanted to catch up to it. I could not worry about position at all any longer. In fact, nearing the ball just as it bounced in, I realized that my speed had brought my body too far forward. There was no way I could brace to hit the ball. As a matter of fact, there was suddenly no way I could keep from falling.

"Instead, resigned to this indignity, I did the only thing I could. I kept going at full speed and just took a swipe at the ball. What did I have to lose? I was going to fall anyway. Then, immediately after I swung, I dived for the ground, preparing to break my fall. I could tell, though, as soon as I hit the ball, that I had smacked it solidly, but only as I crashed onto the grass did I turn to look. The ball whipped down the line, just past Cramm's outstretched racket. He had come up fast and could cover all but about the last two feet on the right of the net (his left). At my angle I could not have returned the ball crosscourt. I had been forced to try for a shot right down the line. Now I saw the ball slip past his reach. The ball landed, miraculously but perfectly in the corner. I had hit the one possible winning shot. I was told later that the ball landed at a point that was less than six inches from being out two ways, to the side or long."

Such was the conclusion to one of the most immortal tennis matches ever played. it was a glorious ending to a single match, but only the beginning of a series of more profound events that were to later mark the certain immortality of the Budge character. After his inter-zone triumph over Crumm, Budge went on to lead the United States team to victory over England, then won Wimbledon and Forest Hills. At this point the noble idealism of Don Budge showed itself to be real, more

than rhetoric, when, at the cost of over $50,000 he declined to turn professional. It was almost as if the hands of fate were working, for had he turned pro then he would never have won the illusive Grand Slam of tennis. As it was, he did capture it in 1938, a feat never previously accomplished and one that stands as an undeniable tribute to Budge as a player and as a man. The public sentiment was so undeniably behind him when he did turn pro the next year that the U.S.L.T.A. officially represented itself at the signing of his contract. Holcombe Ward, the president of the U.S.L.T.A., an uncompromising advocate of pure amateurism, attended specifically to offer his congratulations and well wishes to a man who had truly given more than duty or obligation had demanded. It was a most honorable reception, a rare one, but one that was more than deserved. Don Budge really was an American ideal.

CHAPTER 12

The Killer Instinct

Some players are driven to competition by motivations other than the obvious. The killer instinct is not an obvious trait, yet it is a very human characteristic, one of those fundamental drives that have brought the human condition to its present state. Evolutionists would point their fingers at the past and to the basic necessity of survival through the ages. It is no doubt a defense mechanism of sorts, a technique that prevents defeat before it can assert itself. It is not a preconceived strategy or a calculated state of mind, for one does not wake up one day and consciously decide to be a "killer." Very often, environmental influences cultivate or fail to cultivate this trait—the easy milk-toast road to success never spawning this drive as much as the hard way, the way requiring one to overcome obstacles in order to find reward. The players who exemplify this characteristic are usually great come-from-behind artists, those players who flatly refuse to quit, who simply won't accept defeat. The act of competing is very personal to them and that is exactly the way they deal with it. It is more than a tennis match, for their personal essence is at stake, on the line. Sometimes a mentality of this type will flirt with defeat, never becoming truly motivated until they realize they are about to lose. And losing makes them mad, an anger building within them and directing their play. Playing in a rage, the fury of these players necessitates that they be "beaten," for they can never be counted on to "lose" or give matches away under the pretense that they may be having a bad day or that their opponent is just playing too well. These players have a distinguished knack for winning matches even when they aren't playing at the top of their game, and they can do that because they want it more. In short, when you face a person dominated by this kind of intensity, this kind of will to win, you had better come to play. They know the taste of victory and they like it. These are the toughest competitors of all. They are possessed with winning, with being the victor; not with surviving but with defeating. They are Pancho Gonzales, Billie Jean King, Jack Kramer, and Maureen Connolly.

Pancho Gonzales

Pancho Gonzales is one of the most famous tennis players who ever lived. He is remembered most for the flamboyance of his style and his unique flair for decisive shotmaking. The fluidity and grace of his service produced what has generally been conceded to be the most awesome weapon ever at the disposal of a tennis player. He literally punished the ball every time he put it into play, and he did it with remarkable consistency. Pancho Segura said, "No one is more consistent than Gonzales in getting his first service into play." The pressure created by this kind of relentless and pounding attack was more than anyone in the world could contend with in his prime. He dominated the world of tennis, rising to the pinnacle faster than anyone before or since. In 1943 he was the Number One junior in Southern California, later being disqualified from further competition because of his refusal to attend school. It was not until 1947, after he had enlisted in the Navy, that he got a chance to play against ranked players of any consequence. He was ranked number 17 in the country that year and was to be national champion the next, a feat remarkable not only because it was merely his second season playing on grass, but because it was only his second year in men's competition on any surface. Couple this with the fact that he never enjoyed the luxury of professional instruction as a child and one probably has the constituents of the most naturally talented player who ever lived. Gonzales came up the hard way, a fact that surely played an important role in the development of his indomitable competitive spirit. There was only one means to getting where he wanted to go and that was results, for the tangibility of results could not be denied by anyone. This was a premise that he dealt with repeatedly in his career, overcoming his exclusion from tournaments because of truancy from school, winning his first national title as only a rank outsider, and later as a pro.

Pancho Gonzalez

Gonzales turned professional after winning Forest Hills for the second year in a row, at which time he got thoroughly drubbed in his tour against Jack Kramer. He was taken off the tour, as a result, later being given a second chance at the tune of a mere $15,000, small change compared to the $75,000 Tony Trabert was receiving. It was an insult and an obstacle, but it was also just the kind of impetus required to activate the fury of the Gonzales mentality. He was a child of adversity from the beginning and he thrived on obstacles. From that point on, Pancho Gonzales reigned as the champion of the world, soundly defeating Trabert seventy-four matches to twenty-seven, and consistently defeating the likes of Frank Sedgeman, Pancho Segura, Ken Rosewall, Lew Hoad, and Alex Ulmedo. It was at this time that he was really in his prime, untouchable on the fast indoor surfaces where the speed of his serve was only multiplied. The noteworthy thing about Pancho Gonzales, however, was not his talent, for talent alone would not have bridged the gap of discrimination that he had to cross. It was the killer instinct of the Gonzales spirit that got him there, that obsessive drive to win and to overcome in spite of it all. It was a trait that characterized his career as a whole, but only because he played every match that was.

One of the most noteworthy matches he ever played in demonstrating this part of his character was in the finale of Forest Hills in 1948 when he faced Ted Schroeder. It was no small feat for him to capture this championship, especially after dropping the first set 16-18 after having five net points and losing the second 6-2 as well. The first set had been a classic duel of serve and volley, seventeen times his service scoring on unquestionable aces. Schroeder did not get to deuce against service until the twenty-fifth game. A gutty performance on the part of Schroeder, however, brought the set home in spite of the convincing nature of Gonzales' previous efforts. Gonzales lapsed in the second set, but came on in a fury in the third, decisively winning the first four games in a row without deuce being called once. Allison Danzig described this renaissance of spirit as follows: "Rifled service aces and blazing passing shots and volleys were speeding from his racket in a barrage of winning shots that left his rival helpless." Gonzales' momentum was not to diminish, outclassing his apparent victor 6-1 and 6-2 in the third and fourth sets. But Schroeder had a history of playing five set matches well himself, so one could hardly consider the flame of his desire gone either. The final set brought the spirit of both men to a peak, its drama a lasting testament to the will of both. But the final score left Gonzales the victor and it read as follows: 16-18, 2-6, 6-1, 6-2, 6-4. It was one of those rare matches where both players found the top of their games, a match that pushed a champion far enough to make him represent his very best. It was a test of skill but it was also a test of spirit. Pancho Gonzales won both.

The indomitable characteristic did not diminish over the years. As the "aging lion" of tennis he continually emerged from retirement to defeat the best players in the world. For example, in May of 1964, after having played only one professinal tournament in three years, he surfaced just long enough to defeat Rod Laver, Lew Hoad, and Ken Rosewall in successive days of the United States Professional Indoors. He was 38 years old when he did the same thing two years later in the 1966 Wembly Professional World Championship (again defeating Rosewall, and then Laver in the final). He was 41 years old in 1969 when he sent Wimbledon fans into a frenzy by defeating Charlie Pasarell in the longest match ever played there—22-24, 1-6, 10-14, 6-3, 11-9. The incredible will to win of Pancho Ganzales cannot be fully appreciated by the mere length of the match, although that is surely a testament in itself. At 4-5 in the final set, Gonzales dropped the first three points of his service, his back unquestionably against the wall, down triple match point. Precisely the same thing happened again at 5-6, his service again threatening to desert him when he needed it the most. But the spirit of the lion does not accept the resignation of defeat easily. The following passage describes well the reality of how a classic "winner" responded under pressure. At 5-6, love-40, "Pasarell threw up a wicked lob that hung tantalizingly in the air, the destinies of two men pinned irretrievably to its elusive flight, but Gonzales did not hesitate—his smash crashed past Pasarell and the fourth match point was saved. 15-40. Now a rally developed and Pasarell threw his killer punch with a flashing backhand down the line. For a moment it appeared that Gonzales had been left stranded, hopeless, a strange, beautiful animal dying in the middle of the court. But like some giant conjurer he had vanished into nothing before our disbelieving eyes, and then miraculously reappeared at the side of the net to tap a stop volley across court where Pasarell's fierce, flailing arms would never reach. 30-40. Gonzales served viciously. Almost anticlimatically Pasarell could not control the return and the ball dropped tormentingly over the baseline. Deuce.

"At 7-8 Pasarell had match point for the seventh time and Gonzales saved it again with just the showman's hint of swaggering nonchalance born of habit—and Gonzales believed he would win as Pasarell fought for his last elusive point."

The spirit of Pancho Ganzales prevailed in that last set, eleven games to nine. His heart, his drive to win and to overcome, transcended the reality of his body's years. His win over Charlie Pasarell stands as a testament to Gonzales' superior athletic ability and durability through the years, but it stands even more to the strength of his unmatched spirit, for he is the original, a killer instinct second to none.

Billie Jean King

There is no doubt about it—Billie Jean King is tough. In order to fully understand this illusive and intangible quality one must begin by understanding her motivations and actions off the tennis court as well as on it. Her record on the court speaks for itself, the concrete accomplishments of rankings of tournament wins putting her in the company of the best. There isn't a major title that she hasn't won. She is always included among the best in these unsolvable, but inevitable, debates of all time greatness. Billie Jean has always been a superb athlete, strong driving legs, her speed and quickness of hand carrying her to the net in a fashion unlike any female player in the history of the game. In a word, she is aggressive. Yet, in order to attain a true understanding of her aggression, one must first realize that the capability of her body is really no more than a superior tool, the outward extension of her most personal essence. She is aggressive in everything she does, an initiative that will "take the game to you," no matter what game you are playing.

One of Billie Jean King's most notable contributions to the game of tennis lies outside the record books of tournament victories, for it has been primarily through her efforts and the realization of goals she personally set that women's tennis is now where it is. A staunch defender of women's rights and the liberated cause from the beginning, she has insisted on the equality of everything from prize money to abortion. She is a campaigner, a hustler of sorts, who is good at selling ideas, whether they be the Virginia Slims tour or World Team Tennis. Her password for the Slims was "You've Come A Long Way, Baby," and indeed they have—with many thanks to Billie Jean, the self-appointed "old lady of tennis." She believed from the earliest stages that there was appeal to women's tennis, that the public could and would be educated to the beauty of female athletic endeavor, that the ball did not have to speed across the net at 100 miles an hour in order to command respect. She brought color, and flamboyance and style to the game. She sold women and she sold tennis. The Virginia Slims is now as legitimate a part of the

Billie Jean King

professional scene as Lamar Hunt's World Championship of Tennis for men. The women are organized and they are organized because of Billie Jean's dynamic leadership.

Another more recent brainchild of the King mentality has been the all but revolutionary idea of team tennis in the United States. Team tennis is not a proven success at this point but it does bear the mark of effervescent personality, all the way down to the amendment of actual rules of the game, score-keeping, substitution, and crowd participation. Her idea has always been to bring tennis to the people, to Americans, and even commercialize it in much the way baseball found its way to the hearts of the American majority. She is a staunch defender of "public" tennis, facilities in parks and in metropolitan areas where it has heretofore been unknown. She wants to see the game democratized out of the clubs and brought to the average citizen, all the people, men and women, black and white, rich and poor. She is an idealist in many ways, but her hard work and dynamic personality have a way of making it all real. Billie Jean has gained much from tennis for she is famous and even rich. Yet, in spite of this, and this is all too often forgotten, the game will always owe her a great debt as well. Outspoken and often critical, it is important to realize the substance of her contributions, for they are real and they will last long past the era of tennis that she competes in and calls her own. She is dynamic, she is a leader, and she is the best—a "tough dame" who has a way of winning no matter what she does.

One of King's most notable victories, one that speaks directly of her volatile winner's attitude, was her 1973 win over Bobby Riggs in the so-called "Battle of the Sexes." Riggs, the ultimate Archie Bunker of the senior community, had already hurt the cause of women's tennis by decisively defeating Margaret Court in the first encounter of the sexes. In retrospect it would seem that the whole issue came to the surface at the time Billie Jean's efforts for equality were about to realize themselves. The Virginia Slims were gaining popularity, women were making more and more money at the game; in short, they were gaining deserved recognition and were finally being acknowledged and truly appreciated. Court had completely dominated the circuit that year and was undisputedly the number one woman player in the world. For Riggs to begin his hustle by so dramatically defeating her, on Mother's Day no less, did nothing to aid the image of the women's game, a very real slap in the face for King's feminist cause. It was her cause, the investment of thousands of hours, everything she had worked so hard for. Yet now the validity of it all seemed questionable—yes, all because of a wobbly-legged old man, a shrewd character, to say the least, who absolutely loved the limelight of his hustle, and who thrived on the controversy and pressure it created. The match was held in the Astrodome in Houston, and it was viewed by the largest audience to ever watch a tennis match. It was a winner-take-all affair, and it was promoted like a heavyweight title fight. All the glamour and controversy was there. It was more than a tennis match, closer to a sociological phenomenon, an event that aroused the curiosity of everyone from housewives to hard hats. It hit hard at the heart of something very American, with people who had never held a racket before taking adamant sides, betting everything from nights out for the wife to beer and dollars at the office or with the local bookie. It was an event unlike any that had ever been seen in tennis. Billie Jean King's decisive killer instinct motivated her performance in this match from the beginning, single-mindedly refusing to accept any alternative other than a winning one. Everything that she stood for was at stake. Physically, she began the match in the same way she concluded it, catching Riggs' slow and shallow service on the rise and attacking the net. She demonstrated the true versatility of her backhand, driving topspin winners crosscourt and down the line, chipping the service and commanding the net with quick and decisive volleys. Her speed was clearly superior, but so was her belief in herself. In the heat of high competition and controversy her confidence remained steadfast, the fierceness of her spirit allowing her to play out the bluff of Riggs' hand. And that is exactly what Riggs failed to anticipate from the feminine mentality. It took more than cards to win, it tooks the guts to play them out. Billie Jean demonstrated an important fact that day—that the nature of the human spirit is basically a sexless entity. Degrees of toughness are found in both men and women, and in this particular case a feminine one came out on top.

In 1974, Billie Jean King won her fourth United States singles championship. For many it was only one more title added to her already bulging heap, a stack that includes Wimbledon five times, the Australian once, the French, Italian, and German once, and South African three times. She has won them on all surfaces, but Forest Hills in 1974 was one of her greatest because she faced and defeated her own uncertainty. Rex Bellamy described it as "one of the last defiantly convincing performances by a distinguished fighter from whom the glory was slowly fading." One felt a lack of confidence in the air in her final against

Evonne Goolagong, a hesitation of sorts to the implementation of her attack. As the match progressed, however, her confidence grew, her memory and competitive will overshadowing the reality of her circumstance. Bellamy commented further, "Advancing years had not improved her physical condition, and her active involvement in the feminist cause and the special challenges of World Team Tennis must, to some extent, have sapped her concentration as a tournament competitor." Yet in spite of all of the reasons she should have lost, Billie Jean came from 0-3 in the final set to win. She defeated the most natural shotmaker in the women's game that day, Evonne Goolagong, 3-6, 6-3, 7-5. A champion by nature, her spirit became emersed in the competitive act, her will to win carrying her once again, this time over considerable odds, to victory. The instinct of a winner prevailed in dynamic fashion. Mother Freedom was number one again.

Jack Kramer

Jack Kramer is a man who has worked for and affected tennis in many ways, most of which revolve around his playing and then promoting the professional game. Traveling from city to city thirty years ago was no easy life with transportation, as well as the rewards for success, decidedly inferior to what we enjoy today. While playing the game for pay was one of his obvious motivations, one cannot deny or fail to credit him with one unusual and lasting contribution. Kramer's effort to make the game commercial was the first real effort to get the game away from the exclusive lawns of Eastern clubs to the people. Most profoundly, he must be viewed as an educating factor, a pioneer of the professional game, one of the first to cultivate tennis as a popular sport.

Jack Kramer's career as a player occurred in the 1940s, an unfortunate time in many ways because of the inevitable interruption World War II would have on his development. He played very little tennis during the war years, not returning to the circuit until 1946. He won Forest Hills that same year, decisively defeating Tom Brown 9-7, 6-3, 6-0. He dominated amateur tennis for one more year before turning professional, winning at Wimbledon and then again at Forest Hills. Once on the pro circuit, Kramer thrived. Describing his appeal, Allison Danzig said: "It's the killer with the big punch that they pay to see on the courts as well as in the ring, and the friendly kid from Montebello changes into a killer from way back and up at the net when he gets a racket in his

Jack Kramer (Photo: Assoc. of Tennis Professionals)

hand." Jack Kramer had that decisive winner's attitude we call the killer instinct. He became known as a master of the all-court attack, capable of making punishing placements from the baseline as well as from the net. His pressing initiatives on the court made him one of the first and most outstanding proponents of serve and volley, "big game" tennis. His service was a very fluid hard slice that was placed with pinpoint accuracy, and served to keep his opponents constantly on the defensive. His forehand was a classic shot that he loved to hit on the run. To the casual observer it would appear that Kramer's strategy on the court centered primarily around the use of power. The fact is, however, that while he certainly had power at his disposal, he was very much the scientist with respect to the tactics he chose to employ. In many ways, he revolutionized the strategy of the game, pioneering what he called percentage pattern tennis. His idea was that points should not be played haphazardly and that they should not rely on the spontaneous. Playing the game was not the creative act it might be for a Goolagong or Nastase. He approached the game rationally in an effort to make great performances repeatable. He implemented a theory of playing tennis in patterns—repeatable consistently decisive patterns. His forehand approach shot down the line, for example, became automatic, because he felt the opportunity for being passed was so much less and he was right. He defined certain player initiatives and then sought to make them so good that his opposition's knowing them ahead of time would be to no avail. He was an automatic player who paced himself well. He played at 100 percent every service game and patiently waited for the breaking opportunity on his opponent's. Danzig said, "he was tireless in five-setters because he conserved his energy on his opponent's delivery except when he felt the opportunity to 'kill'." Jack Kramer was a methodical killer, premediated in his plan and utterly cool in his approach.

One of the most memorable matches that Jack Kramer ever played was in 1947 when he defended his United States singles crown against Frank Parker. It was a match that called on the essence of the Kramer spirit to win, one in which he was down two sets to none, seemingly at the mercy of Parker's clever slow-down tactics. He faced much the same strategy that Sidney Wood used against the lethal shotmaking of Ellsworth Vines in 1930 at Seabright. Both Parker and Wood faced power hitters who thrived on the pace of the ball, both men recognized the futility of trading shots with them, and both made pragmatic decisions to keep their opposition from implementing their master attack. Allison Danzig says: "He continually changed speed, three in soft high-floaters, used short-angle shots and interpolated drop shots, followed by lobs that were deadly traps." The slow-down had apparently caught Kramer by surprise, his backhand slumping under the constant pressure of an ambiguous attack. He became plagued by errors. In the first set, Kramer earned thirteen points as compared to Parker's one, but he scored thirty-one errors to his opponent's thirteen. It was an ominous beginning and it continued into the second set which Parker won even more convincingly, 6-2. He had gotten himself into an obvious hole by this time and he knew it. There is an axiom of competition that says one should always change a losing game but never a winning one. Jack was losing then, a change certainly being in order. He started the third set with two service aces and a drop shot, the drop shot marking his change to a more subtle form of strategy with less reliance on power. Kramer's decision to change and adapt to the slower pace of the game was significant for several reasons, the most important of which was that it forced Parker to adapt in returning, giving Kramer a chance to gain the first momentum he had had in the match. With this momentum, he found confidence, and with that confidence he found the range on his hard core power attack. He blitzed his way through the third and fourth sets 6-1, 6-0. The fifth set was not to be a repeat, however, for Frankie Parker was an experienced competitor and one from whom a come-back story of this type would not be written easily. The sixth game of the final set was a critical one, for Kramer double-faulted twice and was down 0-40. With his back to the wall, he turned to the game he knew best, rushing the net and winning five consecutive points in serve and volley sequence. Kramer won this match because he refused to accept defeat, because his drive to win was even bigger than the facts of his play that day. His "killer instinct" told him to do whatever was necessary to win, to abandon the game most familiar to him, indeed to abandon the game that had led him to world dominance. He reduced the game to fundamentals, to the precision of earning every point, one at a time without the glamour of the big game he was accustomed to. Jack Kramer met his challenge, and with it the confidence of a champion grew and found itself. There have been only a few players in the history of the game to have the depth of character of Jack Kramer. It takes guts to win when you are down, but it takes even more to win when your game leaves you, when you are playing bad when it counts. It takes heart, and the absolute refusal to accept defeat under any circumstances, to win like Kramer did. His game was marvelous, but his spirit was even more so, for in it lay the motivation of his action.

Maureen Connolly

The story of Maureen Connolly is a tragic one, for it is not only the story of a prodigal talent lost to injury, but one where fate also destined a true champion to a premature death from cancer. Known affectionately as "Little Mo," she was a champion by nature, one capable of meeting opposition on and off the courts, always with steadfast fortitude. As a player, a darling of her times, the innocence of her youth attracted attention, rekindling women's tennis. She was only sixteen in 1951 when she won Forest Hills for the first time, an outstanding feat in itself. Yet even more remarkable than her youth was her consistent world dominance after that first title. It was staggering and absolutely unparalleled, for during those three years between her first United States singles and her third Wimbledon championship, she only lost one tennis match. Before she was 20 years old, she amassed nine straight world championships, along the way becoming the first woman in the history of the game to win the Grand Slam, a feat requiring one to win the Australian, French, Wimbledon, and United States singles title in the same year. It is almost incomprehensible to think of the mark she might have made on the game with ten more years in active competition. But she didn't. In 1954, an accident whole horseback riding severely injured her leg, forcing complete retirement from the competitive game. Her days of winning championships were over but her days of communing with the game were not. Her spirit never dampened, for she gave her exhibitions and appearances with the same enthusiasm and zest with which she played. It was her way. Rallying with her in 1964 as a teenager was a special event for me, for as she talked to the gallery about the strokes, I remember deliberately attempting to absorb as much of this extraordinary personality as I could. As her nickname implied, Little Mo was small, her diminutive steps taking her to the ball with absolutely unnoticed effort. The relationship she established between herself and the ball was one of utter simplicity, control, and precision. Color on the court was a debatable issue then, but as the spark of her character demanded, she adorned the court that day in a white dress with red polkadot panties. She was so very much alive, so at home in her element. She had a way of totally emersing herself in what she was doing, a contagious zest for life that gave one the feeling that she was teaching the game with the same enthusiasm that she played it, that giving of herself to us that day was as important then as winning Wimbledon was to

Maureen Connolly

her in 1954. It was obvious to everyone that day that she did not pre-occupy herself with the past or live in regret. In retrospect, it would seem that she lived her whole life with the same optimism, the same courage and spirit that brought her so undeniably to the top of the com-petitive game. Little Mo is the most complete winner in the history of the game because her winner's attitude carried her successfully past ob-stacles off the court as well as on it. She was a dynamic winner in both instances, and that is precisely how her immortality should be measured.

Many people today compare Chris Evert to Maureen Connolly because of the great similarity in their approach to concentration. Both girls reached a world class level of play at a relatively young age, and both accomplished their feat through the use of ironclad concentration and a single-minded will to win. Little Mo's loss of only one game in three years may never be duplicated. In order to fully appreciate the incredible difficulty of maintaining such a string, one must understand the reality of staying "up" match after match, every time she went on the court, always against the best players in the world. It is the tale of a champion capable of winning when she was not physically at the top of her game, concentrating on relatively unimportant matches as much as the big ones. It is a story of a perfectionist mentality, a player who thrived on the challenge of personal concentration, who was motivated to play one match at a time, always at 100 percent. Within accomplish-ment at this level, there is no room for preoccupation with records. Her records happened, they were a total, a summation of "present" acts. By giving each match she played a complete effort, she was able to win with unmatched consistency, her present acts accumulating a history that may never be duplicated. Accomplishment of this kind, of this size, and in doses this large, is dependent on two things—the physical equipment to get the job done, and the mental strength and confidence to free the body to do that job. It is a unique combination that always surfaces in degrees, but in degrees rarely as dramatic or complete as witnessed in Maureen Connolly. Allison Danzig described her mental game, her tough competitive spirit, as follows: "The concentration this 17-year-old youngster brings to the court is almost unequalled. Her fighting spirit is even more pronounced the tougher the going, the greater the danger, the harder she fights and the more of a threat she becomes." The killer in-stinct of Maureen Connolly was her defense, a preventive mechanism, the most positive method of avoiding defeat. It was a response of sorts, a reaction to threat, a decisive and positive initiative to adversity. Allison

Danzig also comments, "Few have matched her in quickness and celerity around the court and none within memory has excelled her fortitude of spirit. She is so dead game, so unflinching in adversity and so clear headed and poised when the going is rugged and discouraging, that one is almost tempted to predict that it will be a rare occasion when she is beaten in championship play."

In 1952, Maureen Connolly won Wimbledon when she was only seventeen, her first appearance in a tournament. That has a history of shaking the confidence of even the most experienced players. Her final match was against Louise Brough, a player whose three year reign as champion there had ended the year before because of an arm injury. It is remembered as one of the classic Wimbledon finals, Brough playing at the top of her game, forcing Little Mo with driving passing shots and clever changes of pace. The momentum of the match shifted with almost every game, neither girl being able to keep the initiative long enough to get a decisive advantage. Brough led five games to four in the first set on her own service, a game that tested the spirit of both girls with repeated deuces and fierce volleys. Maureen broke back, however, to even the score with two straight passing shots, one forehand and one backhand. It appeared that the match was far from over even after Miss Connolly took the first set, for she immediately fell behind 2-0 in the second. It was to be a temporary advantage for Brough, however, for losing these two games served only to rekindle her spirit and drive to win. In response, she won six games in a row to close out the match and win her first of the three straight Wimbledon championships she captured before her career was lost to injury. Maureen Connolly had the unique knack of playing her best when threatened most, of thriving on the pressure of impending disaster. Her last Wimbledon showed the same spirit as her first, as fate would have it, again against Louise Brough. She won the first set in short order, 6-2 in eighteen minutes, but the combination of Brough's slowdown tactics down the middle of the court and her own let up set her back 5-2 in the second. In retrospect, she seemed to be incensed by the deficit, clenching her fists and storming back as the tradition of her legend demanded. She won five games in running and the match, for her third Wimbledon in three years and her last major championship. It was a fitting exit.

There has never been a champion of the stature of Maureen Connolly. Her game was methodical, and firm, and it reflected those same qualities in her spirit. She was a rugged competitor who refused to acknowledge defeat any time, under any circumstances. Her championship mentality should be remembered for its completeness, for her courage and drive was a way of life, a characteristic that carried her past every obstacle, off the court as well as on it. She was a winner as she faced the loss of her competitive career. "Little Mo" was a winner even in her premature death, an obstacle she couldn't beat, but one she faced nevertheless. A winner and a champion in the most profound way, we should remember and learn from Maureen Connolly because "Little Mo" was a courageous champion.

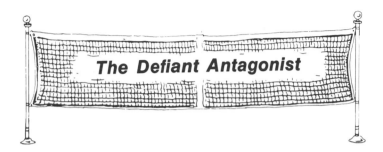

CHAPTER 13

The Defiant Antagonist

Jimmy Connors

There are two sides to every coin and, in the American coinage character, Jimmy Connors shows us that our society does indeed breed extremes. On one hand, we have the cool and poise of a Budge, or an Ashe or Smith. On the other we have Jimmy, the overly aggressive but confident, mature but brattish, prankster. Yet, in spite of his antics, even Connors' most severe critics cannot fail to recognize his prowess on the court, his ability to win, or his present domination of the game. What they do question is his means, the way he wins, the style in which he wears his victory. Connors is a child of American affluence, that segment of the society for which the road was paved with all of the opportunity, all of the external advantages. He was born into tennis, to a pro-mother, her obsession becoming his at an early age. When he was sixteen, he came under the full time tutelage of Pancho Segura, probably the most complete teacher anywhere, a wily tactician, and "Clausewitz of subtle shots and strategems." In short, young Jimmy had everything, the most important of which was the intangible of opportunity to complement his unusual talent for the game. The exaggerated ego of Connors has not sought perspective, his proclamation being that the days of the humble champion are over. Peter Ross Range pinned down the Connors mentality well when he compared him to John Newcombe. He said, "But there are guts and there are guts. Newcombe's are all inside, a concentration upon the certain knowledge that he deserves victory more than any of the others and he will have it. There is also his history of wearing victory well. Connors wears his guts differently, draws his determination from another source, shows his balls externally. Without arrogance he cannot win. He is a man-child before his time, a product of the pampered American system of mother-guided junior tennis, the ultimate spoiled American teenager. And it works.''

Jimmy Connors relates to the tennis ball the same way he responds to any opposition—recklessly, and with absolutely unparalleled audacity. He possesses the most rounded attack in tennis, his ruthless onslaught originating from his ground strokes, particularly his service returns. He has superior eyesight, a talent that allows him to pick up the flight of the ball almost immediately after it is hit. This extra fraction of a second is critical, and it is often the fact that tells the ultimate tale that gets Jimmy to that extra ball, one step closer to that last point of the match. This is also the talent that lies at the essence of Connors' ability to catch the ball so soon after the bounce. No one in the history of the game has hit the ball on the rise as decisively or as often as Jimmy, an ability that stems not only from his vision but from the nerveless, reckless abandon that demands he "go for it" as often as he does. His attack is non-stop from the first point on as he hits, especially from his two fisted backhand, with windjammer force. Jimmy has a great deal of effectiveness at the net, as well as from the baseline, because his natural quickness allows him to get closer with less fear of the lob than most. This ability to crowd the net allows him to hit down on his volleys most of the time, letting him rush his opponent's return since his position closer to the net necessarily eliminates much of the time they have to respond. His speedy eye-hand coordination is unsurpassed. He is a nerve bomb of speed that attacks relentlessly, and he can do it from almost anywhere. Certainly he will try it from anywhere. He is not a rational percentage player. He plays at 100 miles an hour and he does it in an utter frenzy.

Jimmy Connors stands as one of America's most pampered and protected athletes, part of the same syndrome of professional handling that characterizes heavyweight prize fighters. He lives in virtual isolation among a select entourage of friends, managers and moneymakers. He is smothered by them all, by everyone from his mother, Gloria, to coach Segura, manager Bill Riorden, and sidekick Ilie Nastase— Connors' predecessor to the throne of ultimate bad-boyism. In many ways his arrogance is in flippant rejection of the entire system, a statement to the effect that he owes no one anything for what he has, or where he is. He justifies this bigger than the game attitude in the name of independence. Riorden calls it good business and because of it his image has evolved distinctly as that of an opportunist.

Jimmy Connors

The last year Forest Hills was held on grass was 1974. When Connors got a bad bounce from the inherently imperfect surface against John Alexander, he retaliated as only he could—defiantly spitting on the hallowed West Side turf. His act was, of course, by extension not only a spit in the face of the grounds keeper and the West Side Tennis Club, but the whole United States Lawn Tennis Association. He thrives on antagonism and he doesn't hesitate to create it, for in it lies his motivation. He has said, "I like to have the fans against me. I want to do everything I can to get them against me more." With the aid of his managerial staff of loyalists, Jimmy Connors approaches the game like a storm— "through a process of systematic paranoia, by creating false grudges to be overcome, by purporting to be loners and then having the excuse, as Connors once said . . . to show those sons of bitches." His actions run the gamut, everything from unabashedly yanking down the seat of his pants in Hollywood, to "shooting birds, jerking off his racket grip, or giving them (the fans) the old UP YOURS with his forearm." It is his way, an antagonist who loves adversity, who plays to win in order to foil the fans who come to see him lose. It is an image he likes and one he has deliberately sought to create. He has become a phenomenon in himself because his antics on the court have had a way of awakening much of that silent and otherwise non-committed portion of American society. Housewives squeal when they see his T-2000 between his legs on national television, and grandmothers defend him as he humbly praises the greatness of his latest victim. There are those who love him for his nerve and there are those who similarly condemn him for it. He is one for whom sides are readily taken. He is inherently controversial. Some fans feel he is overly chastised, others think he will never receive his due. He kindles a spark in almost everyone and in this lies his popularity, his controversy, his impetus to the game. Jimmy Connors reached celebrity status in 1974 because of his arrogance, because he said he was the greatest, and because, in the true tradition, he went about the business of proving the validity of his proclamation. He is the Muhammad Ali exaggerated ego of tennis, and he is one of the toughest competitors to ever play the game. He literally becomes a man possessed in the heat of competition, a manic of sorts, a total obsessed with the winning act. He should be known as the defiant champion.

Connors was undisputedly the Number One player in the world in 1974, winning the Australian Open, Wimbledon and Forest Hills. Had he been allowed to play in the French championships, chances are very good that he would have completed the Grand Slam of tennis, by winning the four major championships of the world in the same year. At Wimbledon and Forest Hills he defeated Ken Rosewell in the finals, both times in straight sets. Their last match was particularly decisive, an almost unbelievable display of power tennis. Young Jimmy hammered every ball he hit and was just as dramatic and one-sided as the scores of 6-1, 6-0, 6-1 indicate. He was a man possessed, who refused to let up, to take the pressure off, to let Rosewall even begin to get into the match. He began the day playing against Ken Rosewall but he finished it against perfection. He played every point that day as if it were the last, for they all seemed to have a special meaning, a particular significance. It was the most relentless and sustained attack I have ever seen among world class players when the cards were on the table and the stakes high. It was an outrageous display of one incredible winner after the other.

Big business and Jimmy found each other in 1975, for it was then that Connors' first big money challenges in Las Vegas took place. His first one was against Rod Laver and it was played for $100,000. Laver has always adopted a rather humble role as he competed, so the match-up was a natural for the villian-vs.-good-guy billing. All of the contrast was there, age vs. youth, cucumber cool vs. spoiled arrogance. Connors appeared in his patented obnoxious strut. He had on a special T-shirt with a double stripe on the left sleeve that was hiked up over his shoulder in the same manner that a local New York hoodlum might use to hold a crushed pack of Lucky Strikes. Jimmy won the match in a rather decisive four sets. He followed his performance, in March, with a similar Ceason's style victory over the highly touted John Newcombe— this time for a half a million dollars. Connors' method is questionable at times but his results are undeniable. he has proved without a doubt that he is certainly the toughest competitor the game has seen since Pancho Gonzales. He has the utterly obsessive drive that leads players to victory in big matches. His temperament is ready-made for the gamble, for the big shot on add-out, for big money, for all of the cash when the chips are down. He has an indomitable drive to win, a spirit of deliberate and defiant antagonism, an unquenchable thirst for victory. Jimmy Connors is the best tennis player in the world now. The measure of his ultimate greatness can only be determined in time, through the longevity of his career and his ability to stay on top now that he is finally there. When one considers levels of play as demonstrated on a given day, irrespective of records, it is the opinion of this author that Jimmy Connors does his job better than anyone—ever.

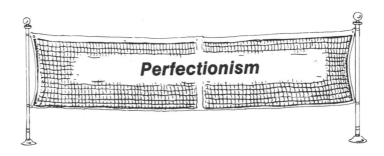

CHAPTER 14

Perfectionism

       All champions are by necessity perfectionists, a mentality they have to adopt in order to compete and assert themselves as they do. It is a human universal characteristic that is an established prerequisite to excellence in anything. Yet, while all of the great players discussed in this book have implemented this way of thinking to a degree, none have been so dominated by it in both method and results as Suzanne Lenglan and Bill Tilden. These two players approached the game as none before or since, and their record of achievement will stand as their lasting hallmark. They were utterly methodical in the learning process, by far the most profound *students* the game has ever known. By extension, they played as they learned, with perfection as their truest opponent and the most fundamental goal.

Suzanne Lenglan

Suzanne Lenglan was a genius for, in many ways, she represents the culmination of most of the characteristics discussed as dominant in the champions of the previous chapters. She was a conglomerate that represented the rational as well as the spontaneous, the deliberately spectacular and the steady, the idealistic, and the temperamental, and the perfectionist. She was all of these things and because of it was the most diversified personality that has ever played the game.

      Many people remember Suzanne Lenglan for her method, for in

much the same style of Evonne Goolagong, she brought art to the game. She was a stylist. Her body flowed at her command, responding to a rhythm and direction strictly from within. Only in the most tactical sense did she respond to specific opponents, for her most fundamental opposition was always the ideal. She approached her feat in much the same way as a skater, like Peggy Fleming, or a gymnast, such as Olga Korbet. Her response was from the heart, always from within, in an effort to commune with her art. She was a perfectionist who was proud of her remarkable record, for she gave so much of herself to maintain it, but, as she played, the externality of her goals was forgotten. Through her play, she expressed the beautiful and approached the immortality of the aesthetic. Helen Wills, who is argued by many to occupy the Number Two position of all time greatness after Lenglan (she won Wimbledon eight times), said, "Her movements on the court, her grace in action, her stroking, footwork, tactics and strategy, and her command in difficult situations in match play were as nearly perfect as one could hope for."

Her temperament was delicate, in the spirit of a high-strung thoroughbred, groomed to race, to compete. There were times that she appeared as the perfect lady and quite the diplomat of France, but there were others where her arrogance showed through. In 1926, for example, she was involved in an incredible controversy at Wimbledon, where she was to have supposedly slighted the Queen by not playing her match on time. It was a highly publicized and debatable issue that revolved around a basic misunderstanding about the times and a lack of communication among all of those concerned. (There was no telephone then.) When she was reprimanded, she responded negatively, her skittish temperament showing itself as never before. "Suzanne, always highly strung, and in any case not quite herself, retired to the ladies' room in a fit of wild hysterics." It proved to be one of the most unfortunate incidents in tennis because even though she played her match the next day, she ultimately withdrew from the tournament and amateur tennis altogether because of the negative reaction of the public and press to her behavior. The strain of being on top for so long, indeed for not losing a set since 1919, was at last taking its toll. The perfectionist mentality will do that, for while utter perfection can never be actualized, it is the goal, anything less than the most complete success breeding frustration. Her mother was an eccentric manager of sorts, and sat at courtside with

Suzanne Lenglan

brandy and sugar cubes for her as she changed courts. She was nervous and skittish, but she was, nevertheless, the "Maid Marvel of France." She was in constant demand, as much a celebrity as Joe Namath will ever be. The clothes she wore became fashionable, and the parties she attended automatically successful. She was a world-wide cult and distinctly the rage of her time. "She broke down barriers and created a vogue, reforming tennis dress, substituting acrobatics and something of the art of ballet where decorum had been the rule. She was acrobat, dancer, a spectacular artist, actress and compelling personality."

The superiority of Suzanne Lenglan's talent, both physically and mentally, so surpassed anyone she ever played that it is difficult to find matches that ever tested her body or spirit. The most accurate statement that can be made must always center around the kind of drive and pursuit of excellence that would motivate her to play so completely for so many matches with the external challenge so small. Her mastery of the external was demonstrated early in her career, her ability to maintain it coming only from a reorientation of purpose, and the establishment of new goals. This reassessment of motivation necessarily implied new focus toward her own potential for perfection and away from the lesser capacity of those around her.

By 1924 Mlle. Lenglan had won Wimbledon five times and when she won her first three rounds without the loss of a single game, it appeared that she was again ready to coast to another impressive, but routinely boring victory. Her health had not been at its best at that time for she had only recently suffered from a severe attack of jaundice. She was a dedicated athlete, however, and one whose personality thrived on the act of competition. She played Elizabeth Ryan in the next round and was pressed to the limit one of the few times in her career. Lenglan had played Miss Ryan thirty-five times previously, and while both were world class competitors of the first order, she had won every encounter they had ever had. It was one of the few matches on record that depict this champion of champions in distress. They say that "winners" are often able to show the reality of their spirit when their physical game lets them down, when they are forced to play on guts and desire and drive. Personal perfection was out of reach that day against Elizabeth Ryan for her body was not the tool of efficiency it had so often been. She played against the external of a body in pain as well as against the previously unaccustomed externality that required she overcome the earthy tangible of victory.

She won the first set 6-2, dropped the second 6-8 and won the third 6-4 but ony by pulling out all of the reserves of willpower at her disposal. It was a victory over adversity more than any, a win many would consider more a credit to her character than any of her endless conquests that had previously left so many opponents so pitifully outclassed.

One of the greatest single matches ever played was held in Cannes, France, pitting Suzanne Lenglan against the brilliant Helen Wills from the United States. It was a match that was recognized as the "match of the century" before it was even played because it was the first meeting of two of the greatest champions in the game. The significance of the match only grew in time, however, for as fate would have it, it was to be the only time Lenglan and Wills would ever face each other. Suzanne had already distinguished herself as the master woman player in the world and, after she turned professional, Miss Wills succeeded her, ultimately winning Wimbledon a record eight times. The match at Cannes has so much historical importance because the two players in question both possess the most distinguished of records, both having legitimate claims to being the best of all time. The Cannes match, and the fact that there was only one, concludes the debate for almost everyone, however, even though it seems almost unfair to put such weight on a single encounter. Lenglan won the match 6-3, 8-6, one of the very few times in her entire career that she was pushed the distance. Helen Wills humbly wrote later, "No woman player that I have met since at Wimbledon or Forest Hills can compare with her. No one has yet equaled her in mastery and skill." The tribute to Lenglan's superiority goes on and on. Elizabeth Ryan, who in twenty years of active competition, won nineteen Wimbledon titles said, "She owned every kind of shot, plus a genius for knowing how and when to use them. She was the greatest woman player of them all. Never doubt that." Few historians do doubt it, for without records, debates of all time greatness become purely subjective. The point of this character sketch, however, is not to debate the issue of the greattest player, but rather to address the method used to attain that title. Suzanne Lenglan's method was precisely that of the perfectionist, most distinctly characterized by obsessive drive to never accept compromise. Perfectionism was a means to an ideal end for her, a goal she came as close to achieving as anyone will ever come. Suzanne Lenglan always sought new personal limits, and by doing so allowed her unique talent to establish new heights for itself, and·an almost ideal reference for everyone after her.

Bill Tilden

Bill Tilden was an exception and an eccentric, traits that were to be the hallmarks of his life. Yet, in order to understand them fully, one must first realize that the paradox of Tilden was most importantly an outlet, an extension of his genius and a necessary part of its expression. It is for this reason that his story leaves one with the distinct feeling of tragedy. In many ways it is tragic, but nevertheless, not all that unusual, for persons possessed with the intensity of Tilden, seem more susceptible than most to this flaw of exception. It is almost as if their genius spawns potential in the negative as well as positive. Frank Deford caught a glimpse of this tragic flaw when he wrote the following passage: "He was the proudest of men and the saddest, pitifully alone and shy, but never so happy as when he carried his rackets into the limelight or walked into a room and took it over. He often lost first sets and appeared to trap himself in defeat so that he could prolong his afternoon, the center of all attention, prancing and stalking on his chalked stage, staring at officials, fuming at the crowd, toying with his opponent, playing the game and reveling in it." Tennis was indeed a stage for Tilden, but so was everything he did. He had an obsessive desire to be other than what was, to express his genius in music or on Broadway, which was a drive that was ultimately to be at the source of his receptiveness to tragedy, much of his fortune, inheritance and earnings being shamefully wasted toward ambitions other than the game he mastered. "For all his intelligence, tennis was the only venture Tilden could ever succeed at until the day he died at age sixty in his walkup room near Hollywood and Vine, a penniless ex-con, scorned or forgotten, and alone as always. He died, it seems, of a broken heart."

Any study of the Tilden character must always depict his perfectionism as a student of the game, for it is here that he first become the exception to the standardized rule. When he was 20 years old, a time when most champions begin to flower, he could not make the Number Six position on the Pennsylvania varsity. Dr. Carl Fischer said, "If you had asked me in 1916-17 if I thought Bill Tilden would ever be national champion, I would have said, 'Whatever would make you ask a question like that?'" But, as irony and fate would have it, he was not only to become a national champion but to assume an unparalleled reign as undisputed champion of the world. He wrote profoundly as a child about the essence of his motivation: "They played with an air of elegance—a peculiar courtly grace that seemed to rob the game of its thrills. There

Bill Tilden (Photo: USTA)

was a sort of inhumanity about it and it annoyed me . . . I believed the game deserved something more vital and fundamental." Bill Tilden was determined to construct a flawless tennis game for himself. It was a process of creating tools with which to compete. He did not approach his talk in an effort to become a national champion or the best player in the world. It rather seems that his attention was very personalized and directed strictly toward a perfection of the most personal sort. Fischer said further, "Nobody ever worked as hard at anything as he did at tennis."

In 1918 he lost in the finals of Forest Hills to Lindsay Murry and in 1919 to Bill Johnston. The Johnston match was particularly significant because it was not only the first of a series of dramatic "Big Bill—Little Bill" confrontations, but because he lost the match as the result of constant pounding to his backhand. It was an important lesson and Tilden proved to be a most astute learner. He spent the entire next winter at the indoor court of Arnold Jones in an effort to reconstruct the flaw of his backhand, to build a stroke from which he could attack. It ws the beginning of all-court mastery. By the time he defeated Gerald Patterson at Wimbledon and Johnston in the Forest Hills finals the next year, he "stood quite possibly in command of the finest and most complete game that any man in any sport has ever possessed." Some people speculate on when the genius of Tilden was first realized, when he himself first knew his destiny transcended hope and emerged into reality. Moments of that kind almost always pass without perception, but, in this case, it is marked, as Deford said "forever frozen in time." This moment came for Bill Tilden when he, after losing the first set 6-2 to Patterson (he was Number One in the world at that time), nodded confidently to actress Peggy Wood on the sidelines, and subsequently won the match. It was the beginning, because he did not lose another match of significance for six years when an injured knee finally impaired his play. During that time he won every singles match he played at Forest Hills and Wimbledon, as well as the Davis Cup. He won seven titles at Forest Hills, three at Wimbledon, and claimed seven straight Davis Cup challenges. "No man ever bestrode his sport as Tilden did during those years. It was not just that he could not be beaten, it was as if he had invented the game of tennis." His realization of himself ultimately bred a confidence of the first order. To amuse himself he would often trade ground strokes with a baseliner, chip with a touch artist, or drive with a hitter. In the quarter finals of the 1921 Nationals against Little Bill Johnston, many people claimed that he had won the year before because of his cannonball serve. In response he said, "I'm going to see what I can do without aces," whipping his famous rival by trading forehands.

The most memorable Big Bill—Little Bill confrontation occurred the next year in the 1922 finals. Johnston was ahead two sets to love and then two sets to one and 3-0 in the fourth, when Mike Myrich of the U.S.L.T.A. said smugly at the crossover, "Well, Bill, it's been a great match." Tilden snapped back without hesitation saying, "It's damned well going to be a great match," and proceeded to reel off the next six games in a row and the fifth set.

A few weeks after Tilden scratched the middle finger of his racket hand on a rusty fence. Gangrene set in to the point of his almost losing his entire arm. He did have nearly half of the finger amputated, an impairment that affected all of his strokes, causing him so much pain the rest of his life that he shook hands only with his left. His career appeared ready for decline when, in 1926, his knee was injured and combined with his efforts to compensate for his finger loss. Tilden had won for so long, and always so decisively, that many crowds came to witness his potential defeat, much the same way the public currently reacts to the dominance of Jimmy Connors. In 1927, the 34-year-old Tilden had put the United States ahead of France 2-1 in the Davis Cup by defeating Cochet in four sets two days earlier, and by winning a five set doubles match the day before. Age had become a factor for him by this time, the previous two days draining him to the point that he lost his singles to Rene La Coste in four sets the next day. It was unusual because it was in this defeat that the public displayed their sensitivity more than ever. "As he strode from the court, head bowed, alone in defeat, the people began to rise and cheer him. At last he thought to raise his hands above his head, like a boxing champion, and received another tumultuous roar." La Coste said later: "At Philadelphia, Tilden could not be beaten by one player. He was beaten by a team." He won Forest Hills again in 1929 and Wimbledon the following July when he was 37 years old. His final great amateur match, however, occurred in 1928 in the first French defense of the Davis Cup.

Tilden had been writing newspaper columns on tennis all during the 1920s, and was a constant thorn in the side of the U.S.L.T.A.'s interpretation of pure amateurism. Almost unbelievably, the U.S.L.T.A. banned him from further play just before the matches, an act that literally threatened United States Franco-American foreign relations.

President Coolidge intervened in the controversy, instructing the United States ambassador to France, Myron Herrick, to announce at a luncheon—"Mr. Tilden is going to play."

Tilden started the match against La Coste (a 2-1 favorite) by attempting to implement his famous power game of forcing drives and serves. After dropping the first set 6-1, the adaptability of his mentality showed itself, directing him to "change his losing game." La Coste was known for his consistency, especially on the slow clay of France. "As steady as La Coste was, Tilden outsteadied him. Each ball La Coste hit came back, spinning like a Frisbee. Suddenly, La Coste found himself playing a better La Coste. On the slow clay, teetering toward exhaustion, the old man won in five sets." George Lott said it was "a display of versatility that has never been equalled. Tilden defeated this great baseliner with chops, slices, drop shots, lobs and power shots, conceived and executed by the greatest tennis brain of all time." Nothing would sum up the greatness of this Spartan effort more than the expression of frustration of La Coste himself. "Two years ago, I knew at last how to beat him. Now on my own court, he beats me. I never knew how the ball would come off his racket, he concealed it so. I had to wait and see how much it was spinning and sometimes it didn't spin at all. Is he not the greatest player of them all?" Tilden himself considered this to be his hardest match ever. "I never was in a worse hole and I never took any greater physical punishment getting out of it than I did in that match. I was physically dead on my feet in the first set, losing it as well as the second set and the first four games of the third set before striking my stride. I was four times within a point of losing the match before I took the third set and turned the tide, but even then it was a terrific battle right down to the finish."

Bill Tilden was remarkable, a perfectionist all of his life, a man possessed with an intensity that may never be duplicated. He was eccentric, and controversial, and so tragic off the court. His is a mark that will never be forgotten for his spirit never died through the years. When he was fifty years old, he played an exhibition with the current Forest Hills champion, Ted Schroeder, and won 6-2, 6-2. As Bill himself always said, "I'll play my own sweet game." And that he did. Bill Tilden—master perfectionist and immortal example to us all.

CHAPTER 15

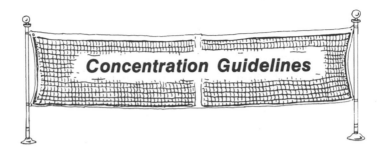

Concentration Guidelines

The phenomenon of playing a tennis match is most fundamentally an act of potential, one that, although the act of hitting the ball remains relatively the same as in practice, is one that spawns pressure and demands positive response from the participant. In its essence, the act of playing a game for score (to win), should most constructively be viewed as a proving ground for previous investment (learning) and a personal challenge in control. "Control" is a two-fold concept in the tennis context, for the winning match performance requires maintaining a positive self image, as well as just hitting the ball. A person's body is really only a tool when he plays . . . a tool to be educated, trained and finally used by the mind in what is otherwise a mental exchange of initiative and response once on the court and playing the game.

Tennis is a personal exercise in self mastery that for many people becomes obsessive. Obsession viewed as intense motivation is different from idle fantasy, or wishing for greatness, because it places work as a necessary prerequisite for its end. Everyone has thought about what it would be like to hold the Wimbledon Cup over their head in victory, but the persons who actually do it are those who set aside everything but their own hard work (that day as well as before) aside, and reject any intervention of fate, luck, or destiny. That person is a problem solver of the present, an oncourt diagnostician and analyst. In general, keeping emotional inconsistencies in check is best done by keeping things "simple," by playing one shot at a time, and from basically avoiding outthinking ourselves. A few suggestions now follow.

Hitting the ball is obviously what tennis is all about. Thus, to do this effecitvely, one must first *see it*, and secondly get oneself *in correct relation to it* so that hitting it can take place. Dealing with simplifying the game always gets back to these basics. These are the points that I recommend focusing on whenever concentration begins to falter. I always, for example, try and become consciously aware of my head actually turning to the side just before I hit the ball. It is from this position (looking straight down at the impact) that you will see what I call the blur of the hit. You will never see the ball sitting on the strings of the racket because it is just more than the human eye can handle. You can, however, see the blur, so why not look for what you can really see? Don't frustrate yourself looking for a stationary ball sitting on a perfect checkerboard of blue and white strings.

Since tennis is a game that revolves around playing a moving ball, a ball placed somewhere away from you, body position becomes of utmost importance. Imperfect body position, of course, means that the player will not be able to establish any grooved approach to hitting the ball . . . and what bad position means is very simple . . . it means that you face hitting the ball from an infinite variety of different swings, and that is inefficient. So, like "seeing" the ball by watching for the blur, I similarly recommend reappraising your position when you see your play begin to go bad. Calculate the distance early and be careful.

The element of "tempo" is often overlooked by coaches many times because it is just too obvious. When players get behind, and their self-limiting self begins to hunt for failure, their physical tempo on the court slows considerably. Everyone has seen heads hang, rackets drop, and feet become sluggish. Can you think of any greater compromise to body position than that? Physical traits of this type are directly related to the mental state of the player. It is because of this that I think concentration can be maintained and even recaptured by consciously reinforcing good physical habits, even down to how fast a person walks to pick up a ball.

The paradox of "tempo" is that while a person's feet should move swiftly in order to insure good position to the ball, it is also important that the actual stroking process into the ball be done more deliberately than ever. The tendency, of course, is to move your feet faster, causing a rushed and more panicky approach to the swing. Remember then . . . deliberate speed for position and tempo, and smooth and easy for the swing. It is a paradox of sorts, but that is when you begin to experience the art of the game.

CHAPTER 16

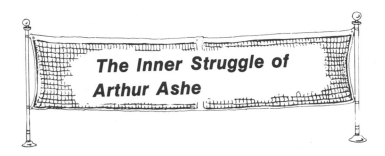

The Inner Struggle of Arthur Ashe

One of the most interesting examples of inconsistent and failing concentration, that for years seemed to be self-limiting but finally mastered itself, lies in the case of Arthur Ashe. Ashe has been a player consistently ranked in the top ten in the world, but whose play, nevertheless, has seemed anticlimactic after his winning the first U.S. Open at Forest Hills in 1968. Players in the top ten almost always have two things in common, usually sharing wins and losses over the others in the select ten, and characteristically making a strong bid at one time or the other to be number one by virtue of winning major titles and matches. Between 1968 and 1975, years that Ashe should have been in his prime, he won none of the world's six major titles. Also indicative of Ashe's mental frustration through those years was his inability for fourteen years (until 1974) to defeat Rod Laver, a man he played seven times in 1972 alone, and at least that many times since their first meeting at Forest Hills in 1959. Hardly anyone in the world would deny the superiority of Ashe's physical game (speed, quickness, etc.), except maybe himself, as he reveals in his own diary.

It was under Dr. Johnson that I learned to play tennis. But he never taught me serve-and-volley. It wasn't his style, the net-game, and he said that I could get it in time. And the serve I did get. But I never could get the volley, not enough . . . I'm not apologizing, and I'm certainly not blaming Dr. Johnson. This man made me a tennis player, for God's sake. But the fact is that if mine had been a typical situation, there would have been twenty other coaches around me, and I would have learned the volley at age twelve. I think I would . . . If I had been white maybe I wouldn't have the drive and the discipline that I have . . . Well let me tell you, when you are this close to being the greatest in the world, in being supreme in this one skill that you have devoted your life to, when you are that close but you know that you will never be closer because of this one thing, this fluke, well you think about it over and over at times like this . . .

Arthur Ashe, from his diary
September 2, 1973

Even though it is tempting to find sympathy with such an argument, it is hard to buy even as one remembers the two crucial volleys he missed against Ilie Nastase in the final of the 1972 U.S. Open. They were certainly not difficult volleys for a professional player of Ashe's stature, and as many have said probably more accurately . . . Ashe just choked.

It is hard to think of a man whose external appearance is so "cool" as choking. After all that is supposed to be such an emotional thing to do. It is hard to picture a man so obviously intelligent off the court and so natural on it "getting an apple in his throat," or "cement in his elbow." It is hard to believe that his mental game could really let him down like that. Concerning this business of image, Clark Grabner said in "Levels of the Game":

He plays the way he thinks. My style is playmaking . . . consistent, percentage tennis . . . and his style is shotmaking. He won't grub around. He doesn't gut out a lot of points where he has to work real hard because he is concerned about his image. He doesn't wasnt to appear to be a grubber. He comes out on the court and he is tight for a while, then he hits a few good shots and he feels the power to surge ahead . . . He does not play percentage tennis. Nobody in his right mind, really, would try those little dink shots as often as he does. When he misses he just shrugs his shoulders. If he were more consistent he might be easier to play.

Arthur Ashe   (Photo: Assoc. of Tennis Professionals)

Ashe, of course, denies that this "cool" is an image and insists that it is only instinctive habit. And he certainly doesn't use it to make himself "less easier to play." Nastase is the par excellence shotmaker of the world and he seems to have found a way to use the paradoxical negative of his image against his opponents. There is more fluctuation in Nastase's character than in, say, Jimmy Connors, whose actions are similar but whose self image doesn't seem to have the same capacity for tragedy and therefore loss. Nastase wallows in his own image, more than any in history (for example, the near riot he caused at Forest Hills in 1976 against Hans Jurgen Pohmann), but to Nastase style *is* victory. It has won as it did against Ashe in 1972 when he was ranked number 1 in the world, and it has found sanctuary in tragedy as it did in 1976.

Pancho Segura suggests that Ashe's concentration patterns may be too habitual, and that it may be too late for him to start grubbing for points by scrambling the way the younger players are forcing themselves to do. The beauty of Arthur Ashe's story, however, lies in the ending, and the fact that it was not too late. In 1975, he won the World Championship of Tennis and Wimbledon, and he was ranked number 1 in the world. Ashe's achievement was more than an external victory. It marked the end of a seven year struggle against himself, against a part of his humanness, and the self-limiting image that attempts to contain us all.

> Rosewall is a better player than me . . . even at his age, and surely for one match. Laver is still better, and so are Nastase and Newcombe. But I am just this tiny bit away from them. Just this much. Newcombe is just a little steadier than I am, for instance. But that's all. I think about how close I am to being the best in the world, and that is so very, very frustrating.
>
> Arthur Ashe, from his diary
> September 2, 1973

Modest in victory, Arthur Ashe is an unassuming and searching man who is happier taking only his obvious due, glad to use his intelligence as a leader but reluctant to be used as a symbol. Sitting with his eyes closed between games at Wimbledon when he defeated the favorite Jimmy Connors, he signified more than any other player the effort required to "transcend" the frustrations that lie beneath his cool exterior. Perhaps writing about his frustrations at not receiving his due (when age seemed to be diminishing his chances in tennis forever) helped Ashe to transcend them . . . or perhaps publishing his writing allowed him to relax about people expecting him to be someone he doesn't wish to be.

Ashe has been able to do what millions of lesser and greater talents have done before him, and will do in the future . . . to realize more meaning in life by transcending fears of failure. This book has been written in hopes of providing new impetus to the common search for meaning through the medium of tennis.

SOURCES

BOOKS

Bach, Richard. *Jonathon Livingston Seagull,* MacMillan Company, New York.

Davidson, Owen with C. M. Jones. *Lawn Tennis, The Great Ones,* Pelham Books Ltd., London, W. C. 1, 1970.

Devereux, Rich. *Net Results,* Pathfinder Publications, Boston, Mass.

Podesta, Fred. *Fireside Book of Tennis,* Simon and Schuster, New York, edited by Allison Danz and Peter Schwed.

Torres, Jose. *Sting Like a Bee,* Curtis Books, New York.

and various articles from:

Playboy
Sports Illustrated
Time
World Tennis Magazine

PLATFORM TENNIS, RACQUET BALL, & PADDLE BALL
by Norman MacLean

The newest explosion in the participant sports world is three-fold: paddleball is now the "in" thing, with heavy competition from racquet and platform tennis, both sister sports. The book is in three sections, each separately devoted to each of the three games. There are charts, photographs, and instructions on how to lay out courts, the equipment necessary and so on. Rules are given as well as professional information on how to become a winner. Norman MacLean is a well known sports writer who has covered tennis at Forest Hills. But for recreation, he turns to playing paddleball at courts across the street from his regular beat at Yankee Stadium.

$5.95 PAPER / 128 PAGES / 7" x 10" / PHOTOGRAPHS / CHARTS
ISBN: 0-8473-1463-4   LC: 76-43416

SOLO TENNIS   by Virginia Yale and Morey Lewis

For the pro, the amateur, or the beginner, hours spent practicing strokes on a tennis backboard pay off in a new accuracy, power, and general shot-making ability. Using the backboard gives you an in-depth knowledge while edging you toward a winning game. *Solo Tennis* covers all the strokes and gives you instructions for building a backboard of your own.

$5.95 PAPER / 104 PAGES / 8¼" x 11"
PHOTOGRAPHS / ILLUSTRATIONS
ISBN: 0-8473-1179-1   LC: 75-36142

SOVIET SPORTS EXERCISE PROGRAM   The Gold Medal Guide to Physical Fitness   by Norman MacLean

Here is the exercise program that has resulted in the USSR, East Germany, Roumania and other Soviet dominated countries producing the most spectacular group of athletes seen in decades. Illustrated with many photographs, the book reveals how the ordinary citizen, as well as the athlete, keeps healthy and fit.

$4.95 PAPER / 96 PAGES / 6" x 9" PHOTOGRAPHS / DIAGRAMS
ISBN: 0-8473-1344-1   LC: 76-16367

Drake Publishers · 801 Second Avenue · New York, N.Y. 10017   1361-1